Talking About Tom Murphy

Edited by Nicholas Grene

Carysfort Press, Dublin

A Carysfort Press Book

Talking about Tom Murphy
edited by Nicholas Grene

First published in Ireland in 2002 as a paperback original by
Carysfort Press, 58 Woodfield, Scholarstown Road,
Dublin 16, Ireland

Typeset by Carysfort Press
Cover design by Alan Bennis

Printed and bound by Leinster Leader Ltd
18/19 South Main Street, Naas, Co. Kildare, Ireland

This book is published with the financial assistance of
The Arts Council (An Chomhairle Ealaíon), Dublin, Ireland.

Contents

List of Illustrations

Frontispiece   Tom Murphy

1. Notes on Thomas à Kempis, *Imitation of Christ*, part of the worksheets of *The Sanctuary Lamp*, TCD MS 11115.

2. Don Wycherley (Harry), Gary Lydon (Hugo), David Herlihy (Iggy), Barry Ward (Des) in the 2001 Abbey Theatre production of *A Whistle in the Dark*, directed by Conall Morrison.

3. Don Wycherley (Harry), Declan Conlon (Michael), Barry Ward (Des), Clive Geraghty (Dada) in the 2001 Abbey Theatre production of *A Whistle in the Dark*, directed by Conall Morrison.

4. Alan Leech (Edmund), Laura Murphy (Anastasia), Mikel Murfi (James), Jasmine Russell (Rosie) in the 2001 Peacock Theatre production of *The Morning After Optimism*, directed by Gerard Stembridge.

5. Frank McCusker (Francisco) in the 2001 Peacock Theatre production of *The Sanctuary Lamp*, directed by Lynne Parker.

6. Sarah-Jane Drummey (Maudie) in the 2001 Peacock Theatre production of *The Sanctuary Lamp*, directed by Lynne Parker.

7. Owen Roe as the Irish Man in the 2001 Abbey Theatre production of *The Gigli Concert*, directed by Ben Barnes.

8. Early draft of *The Gigli Concert*, TCD MS 11115.

9. Derbhle Crotty (Dolly), Pauline Flanagan (Mommo), Jane Brennan (Mary) in the 2001 Peacock Theatre production of *Bailegangaire*, directed by Tom Murphy.

10. Pauline Flanagan (Mommo) in the 2001 Peacock Theatre production of *Bailegangaire*, directed by Tom Murphy.

Frontispiece (photographer Michael Slevin) is from the personal collection of Tom Murphy.

2, 3, 4, 9, 10 appear by permission of the photographer Paul McCarthy.

1, 8 appear by permission of Tom Murphy and the Board of Trinity College, Dublin.

5, 6 appear by permission of the photographer Tom Lawlor.

7 appears by permission of the photographer Amelia Stein.

Acknowledgements

The idea of having a conference associated with the Abbey Theatre season of Tom Murphy plays arose in discussions with Judy Friel: I am grateful to her help and support throughout. Thanks are due also to Marie Glancy, who took very efficient charge of the organization and administration of the conference, and to Riana O'Dwyer, Anthony Roche and Cathy Leeney who chaired the three main sessions. The exhibition of Tom Murphy manuscripts in the Trinity College Library could not have happened without the active collaboration of Bernard Meehan, the Keeper of Manuscripts, and I am grateful to him and to the Librarian William Simpson for the use of the Long Room as the venue both for the exhibition and the opening of the conference.

Cathy Leeney, Eamonn Jordan and Dan Farrelly of Carysfort Press have been most encouraging partners in publishing this book that emerged from the conference. My fellow contributors made my task as editor a very light one by the prompt and careful delivery of their texts. The greatest debt of gratitude of all of us is to Tom Murphy who created the extraordinary plays about which we talk: needless to say, he is not responsible for what we have to say about them.

Note on Texts

Tom Murphy very frequently revises his plays and most of them exist in several published texts. With some footnoted exceptions, the quotations in this book are taken from the Methuen collections with references given using the following abbreviations:

Plays: 1 | Tom Murphy, *Plays: One*   (London: Methuen, 1992)

Plays: 2 | Tom Murphy, *Plays: Two*   (London: Methuen, 1993)

Plays: 3 | Tom Murphy, *Plays: Three*   (London: Methuen, 1994)

Plays: 4 | Tom Murphy, *Plays: Four*   (London: Methuen, 1997)

Grateful acknowledgement is made to the publishers Methuen Publishing Ltd for permission to use this material.

The interview between Michael Billington and Tom Murphy took place on 7 October 2001; the edited transcript published here appears by permission of the Abbey Theatre.

Introduction

Nicholas Grene

As its 2001 Theatre Festival offering, the Abbey decided to mount a season of six plays by Tom Murphy, a tribute to the forty years' achievement that had started with his first full-length play *A Whistle in the Dark* in 1961. At more or less the same time, Trinity College acquired the rich collection of Murphy's literary papers containing multiple manuscript drafts of his many plays in that forty year period. It seemed appropriate to mark this double event with an academic symposium in Trinity, taking advantage of the numbers of people coming to Dublin specially for the Murphy season. That was the origin of 'Talking about Tom Murphy', a weekend conference that combined a series of papers, responses and discussion of the six plays in the Abbey season, visits to two of the productions, and a small exhibition of the manuscripts in the Long Room of Trinity Library. The occasion was striking for the sheer range of committed Murphy enthusiasts

who attended: theatre-goers, Irish undergraduates and research students, distinguished scholars who assembled for the
season and the symposium from as far away as Hungary
(Csilla Bertha, Donald Morse) and the United States (John
Harrington, Jose Lanters, Christina Hunt Mahony). This book
is intended to provide a record of that occasion, gathering the
papers and responses of the symposium together with an
edited transcript of the full-length public interview between
Tom Murphy and Michael Billington that was one of the
culminating 'special events' at the Abbey associated with the
season.

The symposium itself, and the publication of this volume,
seemed the more necessary because of the relatively under-
developed state of Murphy criticism and interpretation. There
is of course the crucially important monograph by Fintan
O'Toole, *The Politics of Magic* (1987), updated and revised in a
second edition in 1994. Murphy is given detailed and
respectful treatment in chapters of books such as Anthony
Roche's *Contemporary Irish Drama: from Beckett to McGuinness*
(1994) or my own *The Politics of Irish Drama* (1999). There was
the special issue of the *Irish University Review* devoted to his
work in 1987 and there have been fine essays on him in
periodicals and books, some of the best of them by contributors to this volume, Declan Kiberd, Lionel Pilkington,
Alexandra Poulain, Shaun Richards. Still, considering the scale
of his achievement and the outstanding importance of his presence in the contemporary Irish theatre, the body of writing
on Murphy remains quite restricted, with much work on his
drama still to be done.

Murphy has always been valued for his searching theatrical expression of Irish experience, particularly some of its darkest and least explored dimensions. His interview with Michael Billington in this volume helps to bring into focus the shaping effects of his early life in Tuam and the Irish emigrant experience that has been a recurring concern of his drama. Other essays here also sharpen our awareness of the social and cultural milieu out of which the plays emerged and which they voice. So, for example, Chris Morash in his paper draws attention to the phenomenon of the amateur theatre movement, of which Murphy was a part, which gave a special kind of expression to post-Independence Ireland. In his response to that paper, Lionel Pilkington details the socio-economic climate of the late 1950s and early 1960s as a hinterland of failed bourgeois promise lying behind the culture of violence in a play such as *A Whistle in the Dark*. Both Morash and Pilkington illuminate the extent to which Murphy's drama speaks the discontents of modern Ireland, the world of the dispossessed 'on the outside' which, as Alexandra Poulain and Shaun Richards emphasize, is so much Murphy's terrain throughout.

However this book also develops another too often neglected perspective on Murphy, the European dimensions to his drama. Fintan O'Toole, in his speech that opened the symposium and the exhibition of manuscripts and which appears in this book as an edited transcript, stresses the importance of Murphy's reading and learning; he gives a vivid illustration of this in Murphy's detailed notes on Thomas à Kempis' *Imitation of Christ*, part of his preparation for the writing of *The Sanctuary Lamp*. Murphy himself, in the interview with Billington, reveals how very important to his development as a playwright was his exposure to European theatre in London in the 1960s. The reference points throughout these essays are frequently not Irish ones. Morash introduces an extended, evocative and illuminating comparison between Murphy and Artaud; Poulain argues persuasively that Francisco in *The Sanctuary Lamp* is a Nietzschean Zarathustra figure; Richards brings to bear on Murphy the thought of the contemporary Lacanian critic, Slavoj Žižek; in my essay I place *The Gigli Concert* and *Bailegangaire* alongside essays of Walter Benjamin. These comparisons are not just locally illuminating in relation to the individual plays. They represent the intellectual and artistic company that Murphy's plays keep.

O'Toole's speech brings out the importance of learning and thought to Murphy, but also the way in which source ideas surface in the plays as feeling. The manuscripts help to substantiate this insight, with their revelation of extended periods of preparatory 'research' reading by Murphy that may appear only very indirectly in the finished plays. In his interview Murphy gives vivid testimony to the intense emotional and imaginative trajectories lived through by his characters that take a corresponding toll on himself in creating them, even in re-living them when staged. This book explores something of what is at stake in this galvanic action of despair and the emotions beyond despair. The metaphysical and spiritual implications of the visionary fables *Morning after Optimism* and *The Sanctuary Lamp* are debated by Poulain and Richards: she maintains that Murphy's is a post-Christian world where 'men are left to deal with their imperfection on their own, with no hope of forgiveness and no fear of damnation', whereas he sees a radical re-creation of the social sacrament of Christian 'agape' in revolt against institutionalized religion. In Kiberd's response to my own paper, he stresses the Utopian belief in self-transcendence in *The Gigli Concert* where I point to its subversive constructions of the self. For Morash there is an inherent tension throughout Murphy between belief and scepticism: 'Tom Murphy's theatre stands poised between a longing for magic, and a deep suspicion of it.' However it strikes us, it is clear that much more is happening in a Murphy play than merely the confessional analyses of messed-up characters 'talking through' their neuroses. In Murphy's work it is the depth of the roots in thought and belief as much as the felt human intensity that makes for the sense of grandeur and profundity.

The fusion of thought and feeling is one sort of distinction of Murphy's theatre brought out in this book; the interplay of language and music is another. The enormous importance of music to Murphy is everywhere acknowledged. Questioned in the Billington interview about the background to *The Gigli Concert* he confesses to the intense envy of singers that he suffered at one point. It is as though music is some sort of perfect expression, by contrast with which language is always inadequate. This is the deficit between imaginative conception and artistic medium brought out by Kiberd as a characteristic Murphyan concern. Yet what many of the essays in the book bring out is the way in which language at its most broken and incoherent becomes itself the music of Murphy's dramatic texts. For Morash this is an Artaudian theatrical language beyond language; in my view, *Bailegangaire* moves from the repetitive self-enclosed rhythms of Mommo's story-telling towards a harmony created out of the contrapuntal interjections of Mary and Dolly. Murphy's dramatic language in its tides of ebb and flow, sound and significance, makes for its own potent music of the word.

'Anybody who is interested in theatre' says Fintan O'Toole, 'knows that the torment of theatre for those involved is its evanescence, the fact that theatre does not exist in permanent form. It's there and it goes.' This is true even of something as monumental as the Murphy season. It was only there for the thousands of fortunate people able to see the six plays at the Abbey in October 2001 and for that time only. The present book, with its theatrical stills, may at least act as something of an aide-mémoire for those who did see those marvellous pro-ductions with their extraordinary individual and ensemble per-formances. It may also awaken the interest of future scholars to those remaining traces of Murphy's creativity represented by the manuscripts – still to be fully catalogued at the time of going to press, but potentially an immensely valuable source for the study of his work. The main purpose of the book, however, is signalled in the open and informal title used both for the symposium and the publication: *Talking about Tom Murphy* is designed to set the critical debate going on one of the greatest of modern Irish dramatists.

Part One: Talking About Tom Murphy

The Tom Murphy Papers in Trinity College Library

Fintan O'Toole

I have to admit first of all that I'm here under slightly false pretences. Looking at all these documents – I'm supposed to come here to talk about having had access to them all – I realize almost none of them I've seen before. Clearly when Tom was showing me stuff, he was showing me stuff in a very selective way, and perhaps that's typical of him. I think he's someone who doesn't want his soul to be plumbed and is very careful about the danger of being reduced to a set of documents in glass cases. I can think of no more appropriate Murphyan metaphor than us all being gathered here drinking in this cathedral of learning. Something about that is absolutely appropriate to Murphy. He is someone who would certainly take a drink; he's also, which is sometimes forgotten, a kind of cathedral of learning himself. And it's the combination of the two, the joyous, anarchic spirit within that immense erudition, immense intelligence, fantastic cosmopol-

FEBRUARY 1973

15 THURSDAY
WEEK 7 · 46-319

Jesus died 2000 years ago but was such a good man that we
still remember him. (Title)

.. follow Jesus; and you will go into life that has no end .... (79)
X : ~~Jesus~~ says life that has no end always refers to heaven, ~~~~
please never mentioned in connection with hell x. hell is temporal.
Y : Eternal damnation.

~~the~~ road to life .. the road of the cross, of dying daily to self (79)

God wants you to learn to bear suffering without anything to comfort
you so it gain humility by passing this business — — — (79)
~~Our~~ ~~~~ wishes sense, but in present time it means bearing
suffering for suffering's sake and humility for humility's sake because
is belief in god).

.. the whole of this mortal life is full of misery, marked with crosses
in every direction (80)

(Since Christ himself was not exempt from suffering) — how can you
~~expect~~ ~~any~~ look for any other road than this royal (80)
road, the road of the holy cross

.. be prepared to endure much thwarting & many a difficulty in
this life of sadness,; because that's how, things are going
to be for you wherever you are, this's how you've said to
find things, wherever you look for shelter from them.
that's the way its got to be; there's no cure, no getting round
the spell of trouble and sorrow; you just have to put up
with them .. if you long to be the lords friend ... you
must drink his cup and like it (81)

— so long as you try to avoid it (suffering) things will go ill
with you; everywhere you will be pursued by the pain you long to (82)
escape.

If you resolve as you ought, to suffer and to die, things will at
once grow better — — (82)

"I have yet to tell him" says Jesus, "how much suffering he will
have to undergo for my name's sake". (Acts) (82)

FEBRUARY Thu Fri Sat-Sun|Mon Tue Wed Thu Fri Sat Sun|Mon Tue Wed Thu Fri Sat Sun|Mon Tue Wed Thu Fri Sat Sun|Mon Tue Wed
1 2 3 4 | 5 6 7 8 9 10 11 | 12 13 14 15 16 17 18 | 19 20 21 22 23 24 25 | 26 27 28

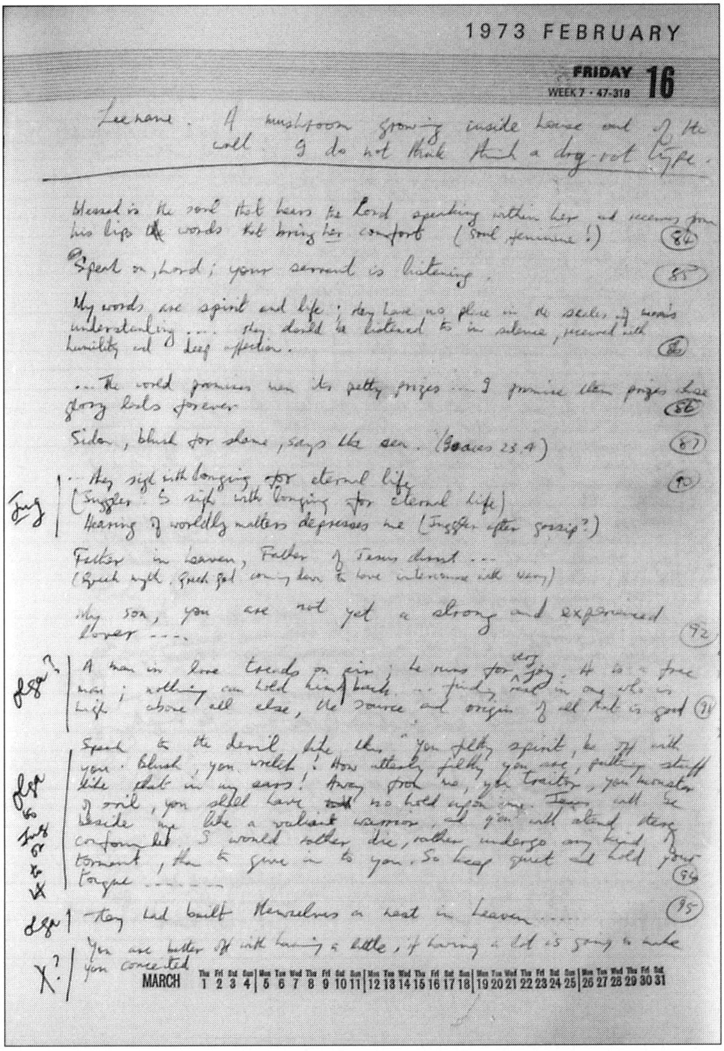

1973 FEBRUARY

FRIDAY 16
WEEK 7 · 47-318

Leenane. A mushroom growing inside house out of the wall. I do not think think a dry-rot type.

Blessed is the soul that hears the Lord speaking within her and receives from his lips the words that bring her comfort (Soul, feminine!) (84)

Speak on, Lord; your servant is listening. (85)

My words are spirit and life; they have no place in the scales of man's understanding .... they should be listened to in silence, received with humility and deep affection. (86)

... The world promises men its petty prizes ... I promise them prizes whose glory lasts forever (86)

Sidon, blush for shame, says the sea. (Isaiah 23.4) (87)

Jug | ... they sigh with longing for eternal life (90)
(Juggler: I sigh with longing for eternal life)
Hearing of worldly matters depresses me (Juggler after gossip?)

Father in heaven, Father of Jesus Christ ...
(Greek myth. Greek god coming down to have intercourse with [illegible])

My son, you are not yet a strong and experienced lover .... (92)

Jlg? | A man in love treads on air; he runs for very joy. He is a free man; nothing can hold him back ... finding rest in One who is high above all else, the source and origin of all that is good (91)

Jlg 60 Jug 61 to VX | Speak to the devil like this: "You filthy spirit, be off with you. Blush, you wretch! How utterly filthy you are, putting stuff like that in my ears! Away from me, you traitor, you monster of evil, you shall have ~~[illegible]~~ no hold upon me. Jesus will be beside me like a valiant warrior, and you will stand there confounded. I would rather die, rather undergo any kind of torment, than to give in to you. So keep quiet and hold your tongue .... (94)

Jlg | They had built themselves a nest in heaven ..... (95)

X? | You are better off with having a little, if having a lot is going to make you conceited

MARCH Thu 1 Fri 2 Sat 3 Sun 4 | Mon 5 Tue 6 Wed 7 Thu 8 Fri 9 Sat 10 Sun 11 | Mon 12 Tue 13 Wed 14 Thu 15 Fri 16 Sat 17 Sun 18 | Mon 19 Tue 20 Wed 21 Thu 22 Fri 23 Sat 24 Sun 25 | Mon 26 Tue 27 Wed 28 Thu 29 Fri 30 Sat 31

ill.1

itanism, which I think gives you something of the nature of the work and some sense of how that imagination works.

Shortly after I'd written *The Politics of Magic*, my book about Murphy, he asked me to talk to·him about a new play he was then thinking of working on, and he said he wanted to write a play based on *Faust*. That confused me entirely: because I had just written a book in which I had said *The Gigli Concert* was a version of *Faust*, and I couldn't quite understand what he was at. But he was reading *Faust*, he was working through it and he was thinking about it; we spent some time talking about this, and I saw the way he worked.

His method of working is absolutely extraordinary in its diligence and its focus and concentration. Essentially what he does, and what I think you will see in these manuscripts as people follow them through, is an incredible process of pursuit. Murphy is an intellectual: he is someone who thinks abstractly, who is deeply influenced by ideas; but his entire interest in those ideas is emotional, how to capture certain kinds of mood, how to use those ideas and subvert them and destroy them, in pursuit of an emotional payoff of some kind. And the way in which he pursues that is through just writing and writing and writing; he writes each character separately, he takes detailed notes about each character as they begin to emerge; he listens to voices, he attaches voices to people; he works through ideas in relation to those characters as, for example, in relation to *The Sanctuary Lamp*. If you look at the extraordinary annotation of *The Imitation of Christ* on display in the exhibition here, he's not annotating it abstractly, he's annotating it in terms of how it works for individual characters in that play. He works through a process of incredible hard work and utterly focused discipline which is quite ferocious to see.

So it was with the play I mentioned earlier. I didn't talk to him for quite a long time when he was working on that play, and in the course of doing that he had been reading a bit of Schopenhauer. The play which emerged was *Too Late for Logic* in which Schopenhauer is the central figure, and with which as far as I can see Faust has absolutely nothing to do at all. So the entire superstructure is built and one small part of it may have been the springboard of the imagination from which the play began to leap and take life. Indeed I sometimes suspect that a lot of the conversations that I had with him, which were very earnest and intellectual, went into the somewhat satirical portrait of the philosopher in that play. So you've got to be very careful about dealing with Murphy; he deals only on one level with ideas and with the extraordinary erudition which he brings to bear on work.

What you would normally worry about, I think, in relation to an event like this, or in relation to the notion of the capture of these manuscripts, is the possibility of reducing that extraordinary convoluted Byzantine process to something logical, to something which is built step by step, and that you can trace in terms of cause and effect. I think, however, there is absolutely no danger of that, because once you begin to look at the process that went into making Murphy's work, what you find is that rather than reducing the mystery of the creation of those plays to a completely rational process, the opposite happens. What you find when you begin to look at these papers and you look at the traces that have been left of that imagination moving over the terrain in search of this evanescent mood that he's trying to capture, is that the mystery deepens. What you can never do, no matter how much work you do on these manuscripts, is to find the precise point at which that material was transformed into the extraordinary audacity of imagination, creating the fables that we have before us – some of the most amazing things in contemporary theatre anywhere. What does remain is the ability to follow the trail to a point where the mystery begins, and that ability to follow the trail is genuinely useful because it gives you some sense of what direction it was pointing in, but never even begins to close it off or to reduce it or to boil it down to some small set of precepts such as a small mind like mine could possibly bring to it.

I think the ultimate value of what we are celebrating here and of these manuscripts is quite personal. To me it matters enormously that an institution as important as Trinity College, a building as beautiful as this, a place at the heart of the city like this, is making this kind of gesture of homecoming. I think it is very important to remember that Murphy is a living writer, and that he's a living writer whose career has been very difficult; that it is not a career that has been marked by universal celebration; it is not a career which has been marked by a sense of being at ease either with Ireland or with audiences or with the theatrical institutions of Ireland or England. These manuscripts help to show how heroic that career is in terms of the sheer quality of discipline, the sheer quality of work which has gone into the creation of the plays.

You have to put that quality of work against the often deafening silence that surrounded the plays.

In the context of the magnificent contemporary celebration of his work at the Abbey – and it's absolutely wonderful that this season is happening – for example, you hear statements that, when *The Gigli Concert* was first produced, everybody understood that it was a great masterpiece and it was universally acclaimed: it wasn't. Most of us who were here at that time in 1983 remember that many of the ways of responding to that play were incredibly reductive and dismissive, and extraordinarily hurtful. I remember reading an overnight review in *The Irish Press* that ended with a line, which I will never forget although I haven't read it in nearly 20 years, 'Take out the scissors, Tom, and you will have the masterpiece you so obviously desire'. It's very difficult to think of something more patronizing and more dismissive, the implication that this was a man who was in some kind of foolish pursuit of a masterpiece, and that all he needed was to take out the scissors and he would have it rather than boring us all with this immensely long play. Most of the discussion about *The Gigli Concert* in public was about the fact that the pubs were likely to be closed before the play was over and how serious this was. This was dishonestly masked behind complaints that people wouldn't be able to get their last bus, whereas in fact what they were interested in was they couldn't get to the pub because most people who went to the Abbey those days didn't take buses anyway.

But if you look at Murphy's career and you look at the very long periods of neglect and the even longer periods of patronizing dismissal, and you put against it the sheer quality and concentration of hard work and fantastic imagination that can be traced to some extent through these papers, you get the sense of how important it is that an event like this is going on while Tom Murphy is still alive. I'm very glad he's not here to hear this: he came to this event on the understandable condition that he would leave before we started the speeches. But I think it is very important this is happening. I think it is incredibly important that the Abbey festival is happening. Too often we end up when somebody is dead saying, wasn't it a pity that we didn't do this? And although he's probably half embarrassed about this, I think there has to be some sense of homecoming involved in it; and anybody that knows Murphy's plays knows how important that notion of home-coming, or that pursuit of a home, is to him and to the way he works.

I think the second way in which this event is incredibly important has to do with the nature of theatre itself. Anybody who is interested in theatre knows that the torment of theatre for those involved is its evanescence, is the fact that theatre does not exist in permanent form. It's there and it goes. A play, unlike almost every other kind of work of art, has no real existence when it's not being performed, and of its nature it's performed very, very seldom. Even in the current festival, it's remarkable to see a play like *The Morning After Optimism* and to reflect on the fact that, so far as I know, there have only ever been two professional productions of that play, which he wrote in 1963. After *A Whistle in the Dark* he wrote *A Crucial Week in the Life of a Grocer's Assistant*, which was then called *The*

Fooleen, and then *Morning after Optimism* – it's that early. If you think about it, if that play had been produced in 1963 or 1964 what a fantastic impact it would have had, how absolutely new and exciting it would have seemed to an audience who were able to watch it then. And of course it wasn't produced for almost another decade, and it's been at least a decade since the last professional production of it.

The sense of this form which vanishes, where the work not just of the playwright but of the director and the actors, and to some extent the work of the audience in appreciating it and making it happen, disappears is something which haunts everybody who is centrally involved or devotes their life to the theatre. And I think again for that reason there is a kind of honouring that is done in the work of preservation, in the work of saying we've got to keep hold of what remains, and what remains itself is finally and wonderfully a process.

There is nothing in these papers that will give you the sense of a finished product. One of the absolutely remarkable things to see here is how late in the development of certain plays they were completely different from what actually appeared on stage. If you look at the manuscripts of *The Sanctuary Lamp* that Tom was just showing us half an hour ago, it's incredible to see that in that manuscript right up to almost the final version there are at least two other characters who don't appear; there are other settings – the notion of setting it all in one place has not evolved at that point. So what you get is the sense of incredible fluidity, of a search, of a journey, which is going in all sorts of directions before it finally begins to come together to its point of rest. And of course what you also see is that that journey never ends, that even the version of *The Sanctuary Lamp* which emerged at the end of that process is one which is fundamentally changed in the course of the next production of the play where a whole character disappears, where the entire opening of the play becomes something different. And you get that sense of someone who is absolutely alive to process, alive to change, alive to new ideas. In looking at these manuscripts, what you get is a sense of how privileged we've been to be in the company of someone who's gone on that journey, or to use that wonderful line from *The Gigli Concert*, to be alive in time at the same time as Tom Murphy.

ill.2

Murphy, History and Society

Chris Morash

Introduction: Beginnings

Given that there is a chronological sequence to the way in which we'll be talking about Murphy today; and given that this talk is the first of three, with the title 'Murphy, History, and Society', I take it that my task this morning is to look at the point from which Murphy's work proceeds. 'Origins' carries too much theological baggage for what I have in mind; 'genealogy' is probably closer; however, I think the best way to approach the task is through the idea of 'beginning', in the sense in which Edward Said once defined a beginning as 'a formal appetite imposing a severe discipline on the mind that wants to think every turn of thought from its start. Thoughts then appear to one another', writes Said, 'in a meaningful sequence of constantly experienced moments'.[1] Since the theatre is precisely this – a sequence of constantly experienced moments – let's start by talking about beginnings.

There are, of course, many ways in which we can talk about the beginnings of Murphy's work; however, I want to try to do so in what I take to be a certain spirit of Murphy's work, a spirit summed up with his usual succinctness by Fintan O'Toole's phrase, 'the politics of magic'. On one hand, no one would dispute that Murphy's work – particularly his early work – is very much rooted in the world of hard economic realities. This is true from his first play, *On the Outside* (written with Noel O'Donoghue) where the entire action (or, more accurately, inaction) hinges on the two main characters, Joe and Frank, lacking one vital, material part of their world: the six-shillings admission to a dance. It is equally true by the time we reach *Famine*, where one of Mother's lines sums up the bedrock of Murphy's world: 'No rights or wrongs or *ráiméis* talk, but bread, bread, bread'.[2] This is also, of course, the bedrock of Brecht's world, summed up in the dictum: 'Bread first: all else follows'. Indeed, if we look at Murphy's work up to *Famine* as constituting a distinct phase, we might say that it is a phase presided over by an ever-present awareness of hunger – an issue to which I will return in a few moments.

---

[1] Edward Said, *Beginnings: Intention and Method* (New York: Columbia University Press, 1975), p.76.

[2] Thomas Murphy, *Famine*, (Dublin: Gallery Press, 1984), p. 85.

If hunger is a part of the world of the plays from *On the Outside* to *Famine*, so too is magic. When I first began thinking seriously about theatre twenty years ago, the relationship between theatre and magic was drummed into me by one of my teachers, a scenographer named Peter Perina, himself a former student of the visionary Czech scenographer, Josef Svoboda. 'Theatre is magic', Perina used to tell us. It was that simple. 'Theatre is magic.' He was right; the theatre *is* magic, in the sense that the defining feature of the theatre in performance is the actor, live and present before us. In assuming the role of another person, the actor is transformed, and this transformation opens up the radical, utopian possibility of future transformations. It may be the character who is transformed, it may be the performance space, it may be the relationship between the actors and the audience; whatever its form, whether realized or anticipated, every moment of the theatrical performance is weighted with the recognition that things can become other than what they are – which, in other words, is magic.

Not all theatre conjures up magic with the same intensity; indeed, some theatrical forms devote their energies to containing it, shutting it down. Tom Murphy's theatre stands poised between a longing for magic, and a deep suspicion of it. From the tawdry promise of the mirrored ball that hangs tantalizingly in the background of *On the Outside*, through John Joe's absurd, comic dreams of freedom in *A Crucial Week in the Life of a Grocer's Assistant*, to the radical, painful, freedom of Rosie and James in *The Morning After Optimism*, the characters in Murphy's theatrical worlds constantly reach out for magic, only to have it turn sour. When the spell works, particularly in the later plays – most gloriously in the final moments of *The Gigli Concert* – we have some of the purest instances of theatrical magic in any repertoire. In those early plays, however, Murphy's characters are too aware of hunger to be other than deeply mistrustful of any hope of transformation. Hence, the closing lines of *Famine*:

> LIAM. Well, maybe it will get better.
>
> MAEVE. No.
>
> LIAM. And when it does we'll be equal to that too.
>
> *(He puts the bread into her hand. She starts to cry.)*[3]

If we accept that Murphy's work occupies a place between the poles of magic and hunger, it may be that our story needs two beginnings: one magical, fanciful, imaginative, and the other material, earthly, quotidian. If so, let's have the magic first.

A Magical Beginning: Artaud on Aran

Antonin Artaud believed in magic.

On August 12, 1937, Artaud left Paris for Ireland, on a mission to return to its native land a walking stick he believed had belonged to St. Patrick. For Artaud, the walking stick was no mere symbol; it was to be an instrument of magic, which would prepare the way for the coming of a messiah, 'The Revealed One' – a persona of Artaud himself – who was to

---

[3] *Ibid.*, p. 87.

usher in a cataclysmic revolution. This coming revolution was to transform more than simply political systems (which never much interested Artaud); it was to reconfigure humanity, including human consciousness and the form of the human body. Guided by his walking stick and his experiments with prophecy, Artaud had come to believe that this revolution had begun in Ireland, but had stalled, stopping well short of its full emancipatory potential. It was his vocation, Artaud believed, to reawaken the slumbering Irish revolution, pushing it towards a final catastrophe that would result in total liberation, freeing human beings from the cruel necessity which is the basic condition of life.

Artaud first set foot in Ireland in Cobh, but quickly set off for the Aran Islands, believing that he would find there, as he put it, a people who understand that 'humanity must disappear by water and by fire'.[4] He checked into a guesthouse in Kilronan, on Inishmore, where he was to be remembered for some time, if only because he left after two weeks without paying his bill. In his room he left a note, written in English, saying that he had gone 'with the priest' to Galway to collect some money. He had not, of course, gone to collect money, any more than he had gone with the priest. Artaud had really gone to Dublin, where he was to hold a series of impromptu street-corner performances, urging the Irish people to rise up in revolution. Not surprisingly (given that unfinished revolutions are something of a delicate subject in this country) the

---

[4] Stephen Barber, *Antonin Artaud: Blows and Bombs*, (London: Faber, 1993), p. 92.

Gardai threw him into a holding cell in Mountjoy Gaol. From Mountjoy, Artaud was escorted back to Cork, and, on September 29, put on a boat back to Paris, where one of the most influential theatre theorists of the twentieth century would begin twelve years of incarceration in mental institutions.

What has this to do with Tom Murphy? Is there some sense in which Artaud had a role in the parentage of Murphy's plays? Before I am accused of making potentially libellous speculations about Murphy's paternity, let me quickly say that the dates don't quite match up. Murphy was born in 1935, while Artaud passed through the West of Ireland in 1937. Moreover, not even someone as confused and disoriented as Artaud was in that summer of 1937 would choose to travel from Galway to Dublin *via* Tuam.

Five years before he travelled to Ireland, Antonin Artaud had tried to explain to a friend what he was striving for in his first manifesto for a Theatre of Cruelty, written in the summer of 1932. 'We are living through a period probably unique in the history of the world', he wrote, 'when the world, passed through a sieve, sees its old values crumble. Our calcinated life is dissolving at its base, and on moral or social level this is expressed by a monstrous unleashing of appetites, a liberation of the basest instincts, a crackling of burnt lives prematurely exposed to the flame'.[5] This is, of course, Murphy's world.

---

[5]   Antonin Artaud, *Theatre and Its Double* (New York: Grove, 1958), pp. 115-6.

'No control over it. No one has anymore', says Dada in *Whistle in the Dark*, after one of his sons has beaten the other to death with a bottle in a world in which their violence and fierce tribal loyalties no longer have a context. 'Ye don't know how hard it is. Life. [...] What else could I have done?' (*Plays: 4*, 87)

I want to explore for a moment the idea that Tom Murphy's theatre of the late 1950s and early 1960s is a Theatre of Cruelty, even if only as a case of affinity rather than authorial influence. From the outset, we must admit that the phrase, 'Theatre of Cruelty', is problematic. While Artaud's manifestos and other writings have been profoundly influencial, his own plans for spectacles such as 'The Conquest of Mexico' collapsed in disarray. The idea really only entered the theatrical vocabulary of the English-speaking theatrical world after Peter Brook's 1964 Theatre of Cruelty season, which included Jean Genet's *The Screens*; Brook's production of Peter Weiss's *Marat/Sade* later that year helped consolidate the way in which Artaud would be interpreted. At the very least, it is worth noting that Brook's engagement with Artaud is contemporary with Murphy's early work.

However, the relationship between Murphy and Artaud is more than just a case of timing. For me, Artaud's concept of cruelty helps to explain that virulent impatience with pity we find in *The Morning After Optimism*, connecting it to *A Whistle in the Dark* or even *A Crucial Week*. 'I use the word "cruelty"', explained Artaud in 1932, 'not out of a taste for sadism and perversion of mind, [nor] out of love of sensationalism and unhealthy attitudes, ... but on the contrary, [because] life cannot help exercising some blind rigour that carries with it all its conditions, otherwise it would not be life … I have therefore said "cruelty" as I might have said "life" or "necessity"'[6]

When Dada, in the closing moments of *A Whistle in the Dark*, protests that he has 'No control over it. … Ye don't know how hard it is. Life', I think we come very close to Artaud's sense of cruelty, as 'some blind rigour', or, more simply, 'necessity'. Murphy's characters, from *On the Outside* through *A Whistle in the Dark*, *A Crucial Week* to *Famine* are all trapped and maimed by this 'blind rigour', 'like a huge tank with walls running up, straight up' (*Plays: 4*, 180), against which there are only two defences. One response is violence, a futile kicking out at anything, including each other, as in *A Whistle in the Dark* or *The Morning After Optimism*. Apart from violence, the only alternative is magic, the possibility of transformation, glimpsed (only half ironically) in *A Crucial Week in the Life of a Grocer's Assistant*.

In this world of violence and magic, language itself becomes a limitation. Indeed, arguably the most influential aspect of Artaud's work has been his insistence on the need to 'cease relying upon texts considered definitive and sacred', and to 'recover a kind of unique language halfway between gesture and thought. This language cannot be defined except by its possibilities for dynamic expression in space as opposed to the expressive possibilities of spoken language.'[7]

---

[6] *Ibid*, pp. 113-4.

[7] *Ibid.*, p. 89.

Can there be a better definition of Murphy's use of language, with its tortured vacillation between poetry and pure sound? Let's take the opening of *A Whistle in the Dark*.

> HARRY (*looking for sock*). Sock-sock-sock-sock-sock? Hah? Where is it? Sockeen-sockeen-sockeen?
>
> HUGO (*singing*). 'Here we go loopey loop, here we go loopey laa…'
>
> HARRY. Now-now-now, sock-sock!
>
> BETTY. Do you want to see if that camp-bed is going to be too short for you, Iggy?
>
> HARRY (*without looking at her, pokes a finger in her ribs as she passes by*). Geeks! (*Continues search for sock*) Hah? Sockeen. (*Plays: 4, 3*)

Similarly, language collapses into pure sound in many of the dream sequences of *A Crucial Week in the Life of Grocer's Assistant* – such as Scene Eight, for instance:

> MIKO (*giggling*). Well, tee-hee-hee
>
> FR. DALY (*chuckling*). Yes, aw yes.
>
> MR. BROWN. I'm the richest man in town but the humblest.
>
> MULLINS. Hah? Hah? Hah?
>
> MIKO. Well, tee-hee-hee.
>
> FR. DALY. Yes, aw yes.
>
> MR. BROWN. But the humblest, sir.

> MRS. SMITH. Craytures, mmmmm, darlin's. (*Plays: 4*, 142)

For Murphy, as for Artaud, these are not the points at which language breaks down, or at least not in any sense in which such a breakdown constitutes failure. Indeed, when a character in one of Murphy's plays begins speaking in fully formed sentences – as the Justice of the Peace or the Parish Priest do in *Famine* – more often than not we see them distancing themselves through the ultimate social product, language, from the implacable necessity – the hunger – which is at the heart of Murphy's Theatre of Cruelty. On the other hand, it is the characters who have succumbed most fully to their hungers, usually beaten and maimed, who speak a language 'of sounds, cries, lights, onomatopoeia':[8] the Drunk in *On the Outside*, Mullins in *A Crucial Week*, Dada and Iggy in *Whistle in the Dark*. In the later plays, particularly *The Gigli Concert*, the collapse of language will signal the moment of transformation that comes only through a complete immersion in unspeakable hungers.

To Begin Yet Again: Radical Memories

I started talking about magic, but ended up talking about hunger; so maybe I need to begin again. Let's talk about Tuam in the 1950s. Tom Murphy did not turn to the theatre by accident.

---

[8] *Ibid.*, p. 90.

Although it was not to happen in the way that he imagined it, there is a sense in which Antonin Artaud was right when he thought that the energies of an unfinished revolution in Ireland could be channelled into the theatre. In the radicalization of cultural politics that took place in the years between the 1798 commemorations in 1898, and the Rising of 1916, a plethora of amateur theatres came into being in Ireland. Some, like the Abbey, turned professional; others, like the Cork Dramatic Society, evolved into more strictly political groups or simply disappeared by about 1920. Consequently, it would not be until the early 1930s that amateur theatre would re-emerge in Ireland. In part, this was because the automobile was opening up the countryside, while in rural and small town Ireland, a middle class made up of teachers, clergy, doctors, and shop-keepers were consolidating their roles as community leaders. A generation earlier, their efforts had been channelled into the maelstrom of nationalist politics; however, by the time Fianna Fáil entered into electoral politics in 1927, the Irish political landscape was beginning to settle into a reasonably stable shape, and people began to direct their organizational skills in other directions. Some turned to the Gaelic Athletic Association, some to lay religious confraternities; but others were forming amateur theatre companies.

In short, the transformation of so many Irish people from audience into actors in the decades after Independence is one of the most remarkable and largely unrecorded stories of recent Irish social history. If you look at the history of any of the well-established amateur companies in Ireland today – not that many theatre historians have done so – you will find that the majority were founded in the 1930s and 1940s. By 1932, there were enough amateur companies around the island to form a national Amateur Dramatic Association. By 1943 there were enough companies in Kerry alone to support an annual amateur drama festival in Killarney; by 1944, after a similar flourishing of small companies, a new festival was launched at the opposite end of the country, in Bundoran. By 1946, there were annual festivals in Belfast, Cavan, Enniskillen, Limerick, New Ross, Sligo, Tubbercurry, Waterford and the Father Mathew Festival in Dublin. Six years later, discussions were under way that would lead to the creation of the All-Ireland Drama Festival in Athlone, first held in 1953. As Roger McHugh wrote in *The Bell* in 1947: 'The main hope of Irish Drama lies in the amateur little-theatre groups of Ireland.'[9]

By the end of the 1950s, with theatre firmly lodged in the small towns and villages of Ireland, one of the most adventurous amateur companies in the country was the Tuam Theatre Guild. In the 1940s they were staging Shaw, but by 1958 they had progressed to plays like *The Burnt Flowerbed* by the Italian playwright Ugo Betti (once memorably described as 'the Kafka of drama'), and they were on their way to victories in the All-Ireland Festival with Jean Anouilh's *Antigone* (1964) and Arthur Miller's *The Crucible* (1965). We also need to keep in mind that only a few miles down the road from Tuam, M.J. Molloy was writing plays like *The Wood of the Whispering*. Molloy's plays, too, were being staged by amateurs, often in

---

[9]   Roger McHugh, '"Too Immoral for any Stage"', *The Bell*, XV:2 (1947), 63.

small rural halls to the basso accompaniment of a diesel generator.

So, we can talk about life in a town like Tuam in the late 1950s in terms of emigration, unemployment, limited opportunities, and oppressive religiosity – and all of those things would be true. Equally, we might talk about the moribund state of the Abbey at the time, stranded at the Queen's acting forgotten comedies by writers such as John McCann in the fading days of the Blythe regime – and that too would be true. But we also need to remember that in Tuam, at least, the kinds of plays that amateur theatre companies were choosing to be acted by and for local people were – not always, but often – plays that manifest a completely unexpected form of that 'radical memory' of which Luke Gibbons writes,[10] in that they offered glimpses of a world in which the harsh rigours of hunger or necessity are pushed towards a point of recognition, and hence of transformation – in other words, magic.

Conclusion: Culture and Hunger

When I set out to talk about magic in Murphy's plays, from *On the Outside* to *Famine*, I found myself talking about hunger; when I set out to talk about hunger in those plays, I ended up talking about magic. I can only conclude by saying that the two terms are inextricably linked in what I increasingly think of as Tom Murphy's Theatre of Cruelty. Through language that veers between poetry and cries,

---

[10] Luke Gibbons, *Transformations in Irish Culture* (Cork University Press: Cork, 1996), pp. 3-5.

through eruptions of violence, and through the *mise en scène*, these plays push our faces up against the limits of what it is to be human. These are plays about limits: life as a tank full of vomit in *On the Outside*, the constant fighting, yelling presence of Dada, Iggy and Harry in *Whistle in the Dark*; the town itself in *A Crucial Week*, and then, in the play that defines the purest form of that 'blind rigour', the irreducible necessity of what it is to be human, *Famine*. However, in Murphy's early plays, this blind necessity is not some arbitrary metaphysical line in the sand; in every case, it is clearly marked out as the creation of humanity itself. Always, Murphy insists, it is the historical product of society – and this leaves open the possibility (even if it is never fully articulated) that seemingly implacable necessity can be transformed. *The Morning After Optimism*, written in the early 1960s, but not staged until 1971, strips away some of the more obvious social and historical context, in order to begin the slow, dangerous push beyond necessity – but I will leave that for later on today. For the moment, let me tie together this theatre of cruelty, of hunger and magic, by returning to Artaud. 'What is most important, it seems to me', writes Artaud, 'is not so much to defend a culture whose existence has never kept a man from going hungry, as to extract, from what is called culture, ideas whose compelling force is identical with that of hunger.'[11]

Here, perhaps, we can begin talking about Murphy.

---

[11] Artaud, *Theatre and Its Double*, p. 7.

ill.3

Response

Lionel Pilkington

Chris Morash's paper remarks that Murphy's early plays are rooted in a world of economic deprivation and that his characters stand poised between a longing for transformation, and a deep suspicion (or, in some cases, a total realization) of the impossibility of that transformation ever taking place. The paper then offers Artaud's 'Theatre of Cruelty' (1932) as a useful means of understanding Murphy's strangely uncompromising and unsentimental theatrical world. Artaud's cruelty principle – 'our calcinated life is dissolving at its base, and on a moral or social level this is expressed in a monstrous unleashing of appetites' – is an extraordinarily useful point of departure. Not only does it convey very well the relentless integrity of Murphy's characters (what Fintan O'Toole described last night as Murphy's 'emotional pursuit of ideas'), but it also suggests the extent to which the action of these plays is governed by an impression of a public world (of political authority and political language) that not only does not meet the ethical hunger of the individual, but mocks, exacerbates and increases that hunger. Indeed, as I shall now argue briefly, the violence that concludes *A Whistle in the Dark* (1961) *On the Outside* (written with Noel O'Donoghue in 1959) and *Famine* (1968) may be seen as an expression of characters' rage against their own social and political impotence.

Let's recall for a moment Murphy's 1961 play *A Whistle in the Dark*. Set in the interior of a house occupied by the Carneys, an Irish immigrant family from Mayo now living in Coventry, the dramatic action of the play charts the changing relationships of the owner of the house to the rest of his family. From the beginning, Michael's father Dada and his brothers and friend behave like Irish stereotypes lifted from a British tabloid newspaper: that is, they behave like drunken and belligerent thugs violently disrupting the domestic order of the house and threatening Michael's wife Betty. The play's action charts Michael's own degeneration and, specifically, his failure to convince his younger brother Des – on whom Michael projects his bourgeois hopes for the future – to re-turn to Ireland so as to avail himself of the new meritocratic opportunities there. But whereas Michael conceives of this prospect as offering a kind of plenitude ('just something respectable, to be at home' (*Plays: 4*, 17)) this is not at all the attitude of the other members of the Carney family. For them – especially for Dada and Harry – Des staying on in Ireland means that he would be forced to succumb to an inevitable position of subordination. Des, we remember, left a good job in Ireland because he is tired of being told what to do (*Plays: 4*,

27), Harry's memory of schooling is one of sadistic humiliation, and Dada has left Ireland because he regards the work that he was offered (after he inexplicably left his job as a Garda) as demeaning and subservient. In other words the family rejects Michael's middle class ambitions for Des because for them Ireland is associated with a pervasive and humiliating class system that guarantees the existence of a social elite to whom the Carneys and their likes will always be subordinate.

Now let's recall that terrible moment at the end of *A Whistle in the Dark* in which Michael kills his favourite and younger brother Des by hitting him over the head with a bottle as part of a savage re-enactment of a family game, 'World Champ Carney'. After this Dada stands isolated in a corner of the stage separated from his sons and trying to extricate himself from blame. The speech that follows has just that quality of uncompromising rigour that Chris's paper spoke of. Dada declares that the violence that has taken place is, somehow, a result of pride – of trying one's best in impossible circumstances.

> No control over it. No one has anymore … Did
> my best. Ye don't know how hard it is. Life. Made
> men of ye. What else could I have done? Tell me.
> Proud. Wha'? A man must have – And times were
> hard. Never got the chances. Not there for us.
> Had the ability. Yas. And lost the job in the
> guards, police. Brought up family, proper.
> Properly. No man can do more than best. I tried.
> Must have some kind of pride. Wha'? I tried, I did

> my best…I tried, I did my best…Tried …Did my
> best…I tried. (*Plays: 4*, 87)

There are several other moments in the play that involve similar inarticulate graspings at redemptive ethical meaning. Although, for example, Dada and Harry both insist that fighting is a matter of recovering pride, neither character is able to explain the exact motive for this: 'A man must fight back', Dada stutters, 'at – at – at – A man must fight back' (*Plays: 4*, 29). But surely the most lasting impression on the spectator in this scene is the way in which an act of brutal violence is here also associated with a passionate declaration of ethical courage.

There is a similar violent conclusion to *Famine* in which, in the penultimate scene, John Connor beats his wife and 10 year old son to death with a stick. As with *A Whistle in the Dark* this spectacle of savage brutality is presented as a desperate expression of integrity. Throughout the play Connor's refrain is the need to do right ('only what's right, I must do only what's right' (*Plays: 1*, 67)) but what this is shown to amount to – at least in a context in which all public and political authority is shown as cynical and opportunistic – is the murder that Connor inflicts on Mother and Donaill in scene 11. Connor kills his wife and child, that is, because his wife begged him to do so, to realize the '*freedom*' which is their '*right*' (*Plays: 1*, 88).

Another aspect of Chris's useful analogy between Artaud and Murphy is his observation that Murphy's plays are marked by a blind rigour similar to Artaud's theatre of cruelty and that the violence in the two scenes I have just mentioned arises because of characters being trapped by necessity.

> FRANK. No, but the job. You know, it's like a big tank. The whole town is like a tank. A huge tank with walls running up, straight up. And we're at the bottom, splashing around all week in their Friday night vomit, clawing at the sides all around. And the bosses – and the big-shots – are up around the top, looking in, looking down. You know the look? Spitting. On top of us. And for fear we might climb out someway – Do you know what they're doing? – They smear grease around the walls. (*Plays: 4*, 190)

My argument is that this sense of an irrevocable and imprisoning social fate can be explained in terms of a calcified class hierarchy coupled with a broader sense of the hollowness of a public rhetoric of opportunity and the absence of a responsive national political authority. The nationalist, egalitarian and meritocratic rhetoric that dominated Ireland in the 1960s, that is, is diagnosed by these plays as a subterfuge for a rigidly hierarchical and socially oppressive society. Ireland's public discourse of democratic politics, of freedom of choice and equality, then, is an artificial carapace: something that is only half-believed in and that cloaks and worsens the psychological impression of inferiority that characters experience on a daily basis. Another way of putting this is to say that the violent Artaudian dramaturgy of Murphy's plays arises from Murphy's perception of a disjunction between the people and the state, and the way that the natural ethical hunger of the people tends to be mocked and exacerbated by the available vocabulary of politics and of public and social life. It is this perceptive disillusionment of Murphy's plays that so marks them historically.

T. K. Whitaker's 1958 government report, the *Programme for Economic Expansion* preceded the first production of *A Whistle in the Dark* by three years. In conjunction with other factors, such as Ireland's membership of the World Bank in August 1957, Lemass's rapprochement with Terence O'Neill's Stormont government in Northern Ireland and the signing of the Anglo-Irish Free Trade Agreement in 1965, the implementation of Whitaker's recommendation that Ireland change to an export-based, dollar-earning economy led to a period of unprecedented economic growth.[12] But Whitaker's modernization programme also gave rise to a period of extraordinary ideological turbulence – a turbulence that was experienced with special intensity in the west of Ireland. The gradual dismantling of the paternalistic state apparatuses of the 1940s and their replacement in the early 1960s by an 'effective consensus for an activist and "social democratic" state' was disrupted by the unsurprising fact that free market capitalism did not benefit everyone.[13] Small farmers and unskilled workers were the worst hit and while the emigration figures for Ireland as a whole declined, emigration continued at pre-Whitaker rates in counties on the western seaboard.

---

[12]   See J.J. Lee *Ireland 1912-1985: Politics and Society*, (Cambridge University Press, 1989), pp. 367-8.

[13]   See P. Bew, E. Hazelkorn and H. Patterson, *The Dynamics of Irish Politics*, (London: Lawrence & Wishart, 1989), p. 111.

What resulted was a peculiar ideological disjointedness. Inter-pellated as consumers within an international capitalist economy, the Irish citizen exists in a world in which the marks of national distinctiveness appear irrelevant except as political rhetoric, and the promise by a state of an egalitarian world of meritocratic opportunities appears to many both as an enticing promise *and* yet as an entrenchment of indigenous bourgeois privilege.

Ireland's class system and its unequal distribution of wealth and resources, that is, continued to flourish and prosper. And although from the 1950s to 1970s Ireland had a higher level of post-compulsory education than Britain or Northern Ireland and while this was due to its extensive provision by the Roman Catholic church, it is also true to say that 'Catholic schools [and hospitals] were structured in such a way so as to reflect, and to some extent, reinforce existing hierarchies'.[14]

This is the context that allows us to read back into Murphy's plays the failure of politics and the failure of a world of public authority, the world John Connor sums up in *Famine* as 'Important things. The Government, the Deal, Business, the Policy – the Policy' (*Plays: 1*, 40).' Apart from Fr. James McDyer's Save the West Campaign in Co. Donegal and the nationwide activities of Muintir na Tíre (both of these political movements were concerned with evolving a more parti-

---

[14] T. Fahey, 'The Catholic Church and Social Policy', in Seán Healy and Brigid Reynolds (eds.), *Social Policy in Ireland: Principles, Practice and Problems*, (Dublin: Oak Tree Press, 1989), p. 415.

cipative form of democracy),[15] there existed little coherent opposition to Ireland's system of representative democracy and its newfound project of economic modernization. Murphy's plays reflect this sense of an oppressive political pessimism. In *Famine* the reason why an ethical man like John Connor ends up killing his wife and child, beating them to death with a stick, is that his utopian desire for a better world is not matched by the existence, or even the prospect of the existence, of a responsive or credible political authority. Michael endures a similar education in *A Whistle in the Dark* when he comes to realize that the meritocratic opportunities of the new Ireland are simply a mask for enduring class inequalities. And in *Whistle*, there is a pervasive sense that while Irish people are united by a shared nationalist discourse, this rhetoric is used by the state as a convenient mask for enduring class inequalities.

Earlier I mentioned that Dada and Harry both insist that fighting is a matter of recovering pride, but that neither character is able to explain the exact motive for this. The most precise formulations that either character can achieve involve hinting that their anger is directed against a vague notion of a bourgeois 'them': people such as Dada's middle class drinking cronies who spoke Irish with him at the club and then

---

[15] Tony Varley and Chris Curtin, 'Defending Rural Interests Against Nationalists in 20th Century Ireland: A Tale of Three Movements', in D. Davis (ed.), *Rural Change in Ireland* (Belfast: Institute of Irish Studies, 1999), pp. 58-83.

patronized him by offering him a job as the club's caretaker, or Harry's former schoolteacher who laughed at his ambitions to become a priest.

What causes the sense of seemingly hopeless claustrophobia is the universality and apparent intractability of Ireland's class hierarchy at a time in which the ideology of the state is re-oriented to a language of egalitarianism and democracy and the way in which, as Murphy himself has put it, personal transformation and romance is completely dependent on economics and class position.

> We danced in ballrooms and, depending on the answer to 'what do you do?' we fell in love. (Tom Murphy, Introduction, *Plays: 1*, xii)

The anger, cruelty or rigour of Murphy's plays derive from the collision between a recognizable utopian desire for an ethical world that is unmet and betrayed by the public rhetoric of the state and the intractability and invisibility of Ireland's ruthless, and seemingly inexorable, class system.

ill.4

Fable and vision: *The Morning After Optimism* and *The Sanctuary Lamp*

Alexandra Poulain

Tom Murphy's first play *On the Outside*, written in collaboration with his friend Noel O'Donoghue in 1959, is a one-act comedy which takes place outside a ballroom in the rural West; the two protagonists, Frank and Joe, are young apprentice workers who find themselves short of a few shillings to buy tickets to the dance; in spite of the various, increasingly elaborate stratagems they come up with, they are denied entrance to the end. It is remarkable that this early play, which according to Murphy was written with no other ambition than to kill time, maps out the dramatic geography which Murphy has been using and developing during all his playwriting career so far. With a few (significant) exceptions all Murphy's plays take place 'on the outside' of the social sphere, in the marginal space of the dispossessed. While the communal order is paralysed by a set of archaic attitudes and rigid preconceptions, vital energy can only spring from those who are excluded from prosperity and denied social recognition. In *On the Outside* the energy and relentless efforts of Frank and Joe are to no avail; but the two plays I am going to talk about today, *The Morning after Optimism* and *The Sanctuary Lamp*, see the emergence of the true Murphy hero: in these plays social exclusion is merely the starting point for the radical experience of despair – a dynamic, transforming experience which enables Murphy's outsiders to let go of all preconceptions and invent their own destinies.

The Morning After Optimism is a disconcerting play, bringing together the sordid reality of petty criminality with the dream world of romance and fairy tales. On the face of it the story makes little sense: an ageing, embittered pimp and a faded prostitute encounter a young Prince and a beautiful orphaned girl in a forest; they try to seduce the glamorous pair but are repelled, and end up murdering them. The play echoes with the Christian rhetoric of good and evil, innocence and guilt, and seems to point to James and Rosie as the two unredeemable villains. The intriguing title, however, warns the audience about the elusive, playful nature of the play. 'After optimism': crime stifles innocence, the world is engulfed in chaos. When the play was first produced some spectators reacted negatively to its alleged darkness, without pausing to consider what sort of optimism it proposes to do away with. The key resides in the first part of the title; the expression 'the morning after', evocative of a massive hangover, suggests that the 'optimism' Murphy has in mind is really a state of drunken, delusive contentment – the illusion of a perfect world, a 'fairy tale' world, distilled by parents and teachers, priests and politicians – 'the authorities' – as a means to keep the people happy and quiet. In the central scene of the play James turns his childhood reminiscences into such a fairy tale – but with a twist. 'Once upon a time there was a boy, as there always was and always will be, and he was given a dream, his life…' (*Plays: 3*, 43). The little boy's dream world is brutally shattered, however, when the beautiful balloons he has been given, 'already inflated', suddenly burst, leaving him to nurse his grief and frustration. 'The morning after optimism' is the moment when balloons burst and illusions are dispelled; the title suggests the grotesque pain of hangover, but also, literally, the dawning of a new day – an image of true hope which has nothing to do with the cloying phraseology of authorized optimism. The play was written at the beginning of the 1960s, at the time when the dream of preserving a Gaelic Golden Age in Ireland was suddenly making way, in public discourse, for more pragmatic aspirations to economic prosperity and material comfort. More generally, what Murphy calls 'the fairy tale' is the enervating discourse which 'the authorities' use at all times to put people to sleep and maintain them in a state of childish naiveté. In this and other plays Murphy's heroes are characteristically immature (James and Rosie chronically lapse into baby talk), and the plays dramatize their belated coming of age as they finally open their eyes to reality, combining an individual fable of initiation with political critique.

The whole play takes place in a forest, where James and Rosie have retreated for a temporary break after James's mother has died. In Murphy's plays grief is always the crucial

experience, but it is dramatized as a dynamic process. To
become adults Murphy's heroes must first lose their childhood illusions and despair of the world as it is, and this
painful process is often initiated by the loss of a beloved
woman – a wife (*Too Late for Logic, Sanctuary Lamp*), a lover
(*The Gigli Concert*), and here a mother. In many pre-industrial
cultures the forest is the place where rites of passage take
place; isolated as it is from the spheres of domestic and social
activity, it is a space apart, exempt from the norms and conventions that regulate everyday life, and propitious to the
emergence of a symbolic, rather than a rational logic. In
traditional initiatory rituals, after the novices have been
separated from the rest of the community, each must die a
symbolic death (figured by various ordeals and physical
tortures, and often by a symbolic descent into an abyss) so
that they can be reborn to a superior status; they can then be
reintegrated into the community in which they will occupy a
higher function. In Murphy's drama the modern equivalent
for those symbolic deaths is the experience of grief, which
provides the necessary impetus for the hero's metamorphosis.
In *Optimism* the forest is clearly marked out as a space apart;
even the little village at the entrance is not really part of 'the
real world' but rather an extension of the forest: 'Still, it's out
of the way, what do you say?' Rosie comments; 'off the beaten
track, so to speak' (*Plays: 3*, 7). The forest is one in a long line
of literary and theatrical forests – the 'dark wood' at the heart
of which is the entrance to Dante's *Inferno*, the forest of Arden
where couples form and fall apart in Shakespearean comedies,
and above all the archetypal forest of the fairy tale, this se-

cularized version of an initiatory ritual, in which little children
are confronted with various fantastic, evil creatures.

Although James uses the phrase 'fairy tale' sarcastically to
refer to the bogus construct of an ideal world (here the expression evokes the traditional happy end inherent in modern,
especially Hollywoodian versions of the genre), his adventure
in the forest is actually structured like a nightmarish fairy tale.
Referring to his dead mother who has been haunting his
sleepless nights he warns: 'I'll lay that dead witch sleeping!'
(*Plays: 3*, 11) – a striking phrase characteristic of James' com-
pact language, suggesting at the same time the raw impulse of
Oedipal love ('I'll lay her'), the rage of the abandoned child
('I'll *s*lay her') and the possibility of the mourning process ('I'll
lay her on her death bed, and hopefully I'll find sleep again').
When James, after several unsuccessful attempts, finally
manages to recite a short poem for his mother's memory the
figure of the witch – the dramatic expression of unprocessed
grief – disappears from the scene, leaving him to deal with
another, rather more tenacious archetype of the fairy tale: the
dragon-like Edmund. During the first two scenes of the play,
James and Rosie are being tracked down by a mysterious
creature which they call 'Feathers', a metonym which reduces
it to a terrifying animality. The suspense thus created is
followed by a comic anticlimax when the inoffensive Edmund
enters with his Robin Hood hat on his head. Although he
claims to be James' younger brother (or rather his half-
brother, since he is really the king's son) Edmund could not
be more different from the cynical old pimp. With his ab-
surdly archaic language and chivalrous attitudes, he is a card-

board figure straight out of a fairy tale – an ideal version of what James might have been in a perfect world, and who may only exist in his imagination, just as the virginal Anastasia is Rosie's improbable, whiter than white *alter ego*. An icon of perfection, Edmund is also, however, some sort of repulsive hydra which James needs to put to death; this ambivalence is suggested in the stage direction which describes him physically:

> He is a handsome, confident young man in his early twenties. He is very innocent, romantic and charming. He wears a Robin Hood hat with a feather, an antique military tunic, jeans, high boots, a sword and a water-flask at his side. (*Plays: 3, 20*)

At once a soldier, a knight, a hippie, a boy scout and the Prince of robbers, the Prince Charming is also, literally, a 'monster' – a fantastic creature made of ill-assorted pieces. To get on with their lives, James and Rosie must first come to terms with their imperfections and get rid of those paralysing doubles.

At first the battle is fought at a symbolic level, as James and Rosie endeavour to seduce Anastasia and Edmund with their sweet talk. Each character in the play has a very distinctive way with words; while Anastasia speaks only in clichés and Edmund covers up his self-righteous platitudes with a varnish of flowery rhetoric, James and Rosie are the true poets in the play. Rosie's is a language of the body, translating intuition and emotion into condensed sensuous imagery. Thus her rather obscure leitmotiv, 'my brains are danced on like grapes to make abortions', expresses a sort of existential head-ache; instead of wine, the traditional symbol of fertility, a whole prostitute's life spent trampling her ideals up and down the pavement has only produced, very realistically, a series of abortions. As for James, although he has none of the equip-ment of the stereotypical poet (he often gets his words wrong, tends to leave his sentences unfinished and can be put off-balance by Edmund's artificial verbal virtuosity), he has a way of shaking up words to produce remarkably dense, unheard of combinations. Thus while Edmund and Anastasia exchange their lovers' vows in a thundering accumulation of clichés ('We are found!' 'Forever!' 'Together!' 'Till death!' 'And after!' (*Plays: 3*, 63)), James' declaration of love is hesitant and self-conscious, but eventually genuinely touching in its com-bination of humility and audacity: 'And now I would like, I would like, I would like, I would like to combine with your sweet self from scratch' (*Plays: 3*, 18). To fight the rigid phraseology of the fairy tale, embodied by the young couple, James and Rosie recreate a language of their own – 'off the beaten track'. However, to get rid of Edmund and Anastasia for real, they will have to confront them physically as well as linguistically.

At the beginning of the play several features of James and Rosie are deliberately ill-defined. Murphy questions his characters' identities by playing with their names: while Edmund and Anastasia gorge themselves comically on the repetition of each other's name, James and Rosie's identities are shown to be vague and changeable. In an attempt to mis-lead Edmund James gives himself a fake name, and later fails to have his true identity recognized. As to Rosie, according to whether she is perceived as a prostitute, remembered as a young girl, idealized as a saint or allegorized as a fragile flower, she is addressed variously as Rosie, Mary Rose, Mary or Rose. At a social level James and Rosie's status is equally ill-defined. A pimp and a prostitute, they occupy an ambiguous position in the social order: they are neither 'respectable' citizens integrated in society, nor criminals working against it, but belong to a peripheral area 'on the outside' – a blurred, impoverished margin which has no share in prosperity. Besides, the contrast between their social origins marginalizes them even further; Rosie, whose father is a magistrate and whose uncle is a bishop, is a daughter of the bourgeoisie who has been seduced by a 'tough' – an unacceptable union according to the social conventions of 1960s Ireland. In a different context this might have produced a melodramatic effect – an Irish version of *Love Story*, which *Optimism* parodies to some extent – but clearly for some time James and Rosie's relationship has been based on commerce rather than romance. The couple thus simply remains a social oddity, fitting in no pre-existing category. To escape this social limbo and achieve a firm identity, James and Rosie have no choice but to embrace their condition as outsiders and radicalize it. As they have long since forfeited any claims to 'respectability' (not the most enviable quality in Murphy's view) their only option is to strive the other way; describing himself in the third person, James calls himself 'a mean-un' and claims 'that he is a volunteer for dirty deeds, that he's mightily proud of getting worse, that he aims to hit rock-bottom, for his basis' (*Plays: 3*, 49).

The initiatory motif of the descent into the abyss is here given a fresh meaning, transposed as it is into the context of a moral geography: according to the Christian world view vice and virtue stand at opposite poles on a vertical axis – only here salvation is to be sought downwards, at the bottom of the abyss. To 'hit rock bottom' James and Rosie will commit the one deed for which they can never be forgiven, and murder their fairy tale doubles in cold blood. If Rosie stabs Anastasia off-stage, James's assault on his brother takes place in full view of the audience, and is choreographed as a scene of deliberate, gratuitous brutality: James fights Edmund in a duel and disarms him, but affects to take pity on him and embraces him, the better to stab him in the back. With this treacherous gesture he deprives his deed of any legitimacy and rejects any 'attenuating circumstances' that might have been conceded in the event of a fair fight. By killing Edmund James gets rid of the Innocent in himself, thereby discovering what he really is: 'Now I know who you are', Edmund rejoices as he receives James' treacherous embrace; 'Now you can be sure of it' James retorts, stabbing him in the back (*Plays: 3*, 95). In this spectacular dramatization of the mirror stage the murder might be symbolic, but the psychic violence involved in the process is made very palpable on stage, and gives the play its remarkable energy. Contrary to the traditional formulaic ending of fairy tales, the final speeches, spoken by James and Rosie through their tears, are pointedly inconclusive:

ROSIE. We done it James.

JAMES. We did.

ROSIE. What have we done?

JAMES. We'll see.

ROSIE. It's nice to cry, James.

JAMES. Don't be fooled by it, Rosie.

ROSIE. You can't trust it, James.

JAMES. We might be laughing in a minute. (*Plays: 3*, 96)

With Edmund and Anastasia all certainties, all ready-made representations have been swept away; the two heroes might not live happily ever after, but they have retrieved a capacity to feel basic emotions, and as they emerge from the forest their names, which they repeat in a muted litany, have at least acquired a new stability.

With *Sanctuary Lamp* Murphy takes his reflection on preconceptions and imposed ideologies one step further, and addresses the sensitive issue of religion. When the play was first staged in 1975 at the Abbey, part of the audience was outraged by its violent attacks on the Catholic Church which one character, Francisco, describes as a colossal propaganda machine. The memorable controversy that ensued, however, tended to obscure the issue. Certainly Murphy has little sympathy for the Catholic Church; yet Francisco is just one character in the play, and by no means the playwright's mouthpiece. Rather than a polemic attack on one institution, what is at stake in *Sanctuary Lamp* is a philosophical questioning of the idea of God, and of the role it can or cannot play in modern societies. The play takes place inside a Catholic church, probably in England: like the forest in *Optimism*, the church is a liminal space where the rules of the outside world are suspended – a theatrical space where individual destinies can be played out. With the 'sanctuary lamp' in its centre, the house of God is a representation of the macrocosm organized around the figure of the divinity – a conception which is not specific to Christianity, but which finds its counterpart in all agricultural civilizations. In this particular church, however, Harry, the down-and-out Jew and ex-circus-strongman who has been hired as church clerk, remarks that 'the roof is falling in': in modern times the traditional world picture is crumbling down, and the role attributed to the figure of God needs to be re-assessed.

At one level, undeniably, Murphy settles his account with the Catholic Church. Francisco, an Irish Catholic who was educated by the Jesuits, is ferociously anticlerical. Although he claims to have forgotten everything he might have learnt from his teachers, Francisco has internalized their rhetorical weaponry and speaks in long, scathing tirades, often structured as sermons – and he uses his verbal skills to vilify their methods of intimidation, describing them as a purely repressive body and comparing them to the Furies, the goddesses of revenge in Greek mythology. However, the one priest character in the play, the kindly Monsignor who offers Harry shelter and a job at the church, has little in common with Francisco's fanatical Furies; actually, long before Francisco's first appearance, the questioning of the religious institution has already started 'from within', thanks to the Monsignor's disillusioned approach to the Catholic faith. As he instructs Harry in his new duties as church clerk in the opening scene, it appears that to him all the elements of the cult he is in charge of are only material, even trivial details, devoid of any spiritual significance. To him the Sanctuary Lamp merely 'signifies' the Constant Presence (it is a metaphor rather than a literal manifestation of God) and while Harry is fascinated by its 'mystery' all that preoccupies the Monsignor is that Harry should 'replace the candle every twenty-four hours or so.' An enlightened humanist, he affects a slightly sarcastic indifference towards various aspects of the Christian dogma and ecclesiastic hierarchy, even passing frankly disrespectful remarks on the Pope. Although the Monsignor displays a true Christian spirit, spontaneously offering to help out Harry and providing a dramatic counterpoint to the 'Furies', he has become alienated from the Church he represents, which tends to give precedence to ritual, and forget the Christian ideal of charity and tolerance.

By casting a doubt on the legitimacy of the Catholic Church Murphy creates a climate of anxiety in which more fundamental questions may be raised. Harry, whom Francisco describes as 'a half-lapsed Jew', has come to the church to seek shelter after his wife Olga was seduced by his best friend Francisco, and their daughter Teresa died in his own arms – a tragedy which has drained him of his once legendary strength. Racked by guilt and resentment, he addresses the Sanctuary Lamp in a confused soliloquy, asking alternatively for forgetfulness or for the will to carry out his revenge. The speech is a desperate attempt to ascertain that there still is a God, and that chaos has not entirely taken over; the dramatic intensity of the scene comes from the conversational style of Harry's tirade, met by the Lamp's obstinate silence. The same silence greets Maudie, an orphaned adolescent mother who has also lost her child and has come to the church to ask for 'forgiveness'. While the divine presence fails to manifest itself, it is Francisco who appears to preach his sacrilegious gospel to Harry and Maudie.

Francisco is an Irish Zarathustra who uses the tropes of pulpit rhetoric to preach the death of God. Like Nietzsche's poet-prophet, he denies the existence of a superior being that might hold the cosmos together, and pass a judgement on men: 'There's no one to bless you', he claims; 'And worse, there's no one to curse you' (*Plays: 3*, 156). Thus, men are left to deal with their imperfection on their own, with no hope of forgiveness and no fear of damnation, and only those who accept their finitude stand a chance of fulfilling their human destiny. With distinctly Nietzschean accents Francisco subverts the very foundations of Christian morality:

> I have a dream, I have a dream! The day is coming, the second coming, the final judgement, the not too distant future, before that simple light of man: when Jesus, Man, total man, will call to his side the goats – 'Come ye blessed!' Yea, call to his side all those rakish, dissolute, suicidal, fornicating goats, taken in adultery and what-have-you. And proclaim to the coonics, blush for shame, you blackguards, be off with you, you wretches, depart from me ye accursed complicated affliction! And that, my dear brother and sister, is my dream, my hope, my vision and my belief. (*Plays: 3*, 155)

As in *Optimism*, the only path to individual salvation runs through the Christian Hell – an initiatory *locus* rather than a final, moral destination. Francisco has not come just to preach to Harry, however, but also to tell him that Olga is dead – partly through Harry's own fault. In the play's most intense passage Francisco, perched on the pulpit and out of Harry's reach, delivers the story of 'the critic's ball' – how Francisco, Olga and the dwarf Sam, all of them circus performers, bungled their final engagement after Harry had walked out on them in a weak attempt at revenge. The story is a droll improvisation in vaudeville style, but the tragic conclusion (how Olga couldn't live down the humiliation and died from an overdose) is left out for Harry to infer. In Murphy's drama speech is never used as a mere ideological instrument, but as a driving force: while the tragedy of Teresa's death had paralysed him, the loss of Olga, for which he is partly responsible, jolts him out of his stupor and restores him to his former strength. In the first act, before Francisco's entrance, Harry had tried in vain to lift the heavy pulpit, and reflected bitterly upon his bygone glory: 'I'd have waltzed around the floor with that' (*Plays: 3*, 109). By the end of Francisco's story, he lifts the pulpit at arm's length with Francisco in it – a Nietzschean superman born of despair and the recognition that guilt must be borne without the comforting prospect of a judgement passed from above. This rather childish *tour de force* is in fact a truly subversive gesture, which challenges the authority of the pulpit – or of any discourse that imposes a worldview revolving around the figure of God – and opens new possibilities.

In the final stage of the play, after Francisco and Harry's reconciliation, the latter offers his own version of life after death:

> HARRY: The soul – y'know? – like a silhouette. And when you die it moves out into … slow-moving mists of space and time. Awake in oblivion actually. And it moves out from the world to take its place in the silent outer wall of eternity. The wall that keeps all those moving mists of time and space together. (*Plays: 3*, 158)

The image of the 'wall of silhouettes' springs only from Harry's imagination: no reference is made to a superior power that might decide on the soul's fate after death; even the standard term 'soul' is abandoned in favour of 'silhouette', a simple, essentially visual word devoid of any moral or meta-physical connotation. While Francisco deconstructs the text of Catholicism, using its tropes of predilection to turn its value system on its head, Harry writes his own text, recognizing no allegiance to any preconceived dogma.

I remember asking Tom Hickey, who first played the role of JPW in *Gigli*, if he had felt there was a specific difficulty in that play in terms of acting. 'Yes', he said, 'it's got lots of words in it.' Certainly Murphy's drama is word-based and extraordinarily word-conscious: each character has a language of his/her own, and scripts are composed like opera libretti, where words are treated as musical material and sound and rhythm are primordial. Yet one constant preoccupation of this drama is to shake up words, to challenge the texts which keep communities together and keep them under control. At one level Murphy's plays are all exercises in disarticulation – a process which can only be attempted 'on the outside', and which paves the way for an individual re-appropriation of language.

ill.5

Response

Shaun Richards

Alexandra usefully points out to us the liminal locations of *The Morning After Optimism* and *The Sanctuary Lamp* – the forest and the church respectively. And of course the social origins of English language theatre itself – that of Elizabethan England – were also liminal; outside the city walls of London, neighbouring bear pits and brothels in the area known as the Liberties because they were effectively 'at liberty' from both Crown and city sheriffs. Here were also found the lazar houses, leper hostels, and that proximity of disease and theatre is significant, for the theatre, like the lepers, was regarded as a source of infection, dangerous to the stability of the physical and the social body. It is perhaps difficult to register such perceptions of the sheer power of the theatre in a context where even socially conscious, serious theatre, is part of the culinary experience of consumption. But that serious, fundamental aspect of theatre is what Tom Murphy returns us to, not in terms of where his theatre is located, but in terms of the liminal world and issues he addresses. For his characters, to quote Alexandra, are also from 'the marginal sphere of the dispossessed'. A 'marginal' and, I would add, a desolate sphere. This is a desolation of the dispossessed which is as surely metaphysical as it is social: when Harry says to Maudie in *The Sanctuary Lamp*: 'Maudie, would you like --' she breaks in with 'Forgiveness. Forgiveness' (*Plays: 3*, 121). And when Francisco denies its possibility 'There's no such thing as forgiveness', her response is a simple, repeated, 'There is' (*Plays: 3*, 129).

While Murphy is centrally an Irish playwright in terms of the location of the majority of his plays and certainly his overt themes and characters, the liminal locations of *Morning After Optimism* and *Sanctuary Lamp* lack that specificity. The forest of *The Morning After Optimism* is given as simply 'a forest' (*Plays: 3*, 5) and in the fairy tale/fantasy world of the play, with the exception of a brief reference to the possibility of rowing to Japan or Europe, we lack concrete geographical referents to enable us to locate this forest, to ground it in a specific social and historical frame. The world of *Sanctuary Lamp* is more clearly that of a recognizable society; when Harry enters with fish and chips, for instance, we accept the convention that what we are seeing on stage is but a fragment of the wider off-stage world from which characters enter and to which they return. Likewise we accept the existence of the pre-play world to which they refer. We then are seeing a moment in time and a fragment of a social totality. But as to where this is, the stage directions state simply 'a church in a city' (*Plays: 3*, 97), and while the critical consensus is that this is England there's nothing that narrows this down beyond that possibility. Moreover, there is nothing specifically, overtly Irish. But there is, to take Raymond Williams's term, a 'structure of feeling', a sensibility, a mood. And it's this, of course, which forms the basis for Alexandra's statement with regard to *The Morning After Optimism* that it 'was written at the beginning of the 1960s, at the time when the dream of preserving a Gaelic Golden Age in Ireland was suddenly making way, in public discourse, for more pragmatic aspirations to economic prosperity and material comfort.' This is a classic Murphy concern overtly addressed in *Conversations on a Homecoming* and Tom's agonized perception that Ireland is for sale 'to any old bidder with a pound, a dollar, a mark or a yen.' (*Plays: 2*, 80)

We could, of course, look to *Sanctuary Lamp* and recognize that despite its geographical imprecision it does have specificity with regard to a social institution, namely that of the Catholic Church whose perceived inadequacies are so lengthily and brutally addressed by Francisco, the one Irish character of the play. And that here, perhaps, we have not simply a social concern but an Irish social concern. But what is denounced are not the social practices of bishops or priests which have become the matter of public debate since Murphy wrote the play. Rather what is addressed here is the inadequacy of Catholic, Christian teaching to sustain, to make whole — and it's wholeness that the characters are searching for. But not a wholeness which is pre-determined, pre-packaged, handed down by 'authority'. In these two plays 'authority' must be overthrown. So in *Morning After Optimism*

James, to quote from Fintan O'Toole's study of Murphy, is 'pitched against both the dragon and the witch, the father and the mother'[16], a point which Alexandra too makes when she speaks of James's final ability to recite a poem for his mother's memory, so enabling the witch to disappear from the scene. In *Sanctuary Lamp* the parental figure is the absolute figure of God. But while, according to Francisco, 'God made the world, right?, and fair play to him. What has he done since? Tell me. Right, I'll tell you. Evaporated himself. When they painted his toenails and turned him into a church he lost his ambition, gave up learning, stagnated for a while, then gave up even that, said fuck it, forget it, and became a vague pain in his own and everybody else's arse.' (*Plays: 3*, 128) God is then perhaps not so much dead as absent, ineffectual. Displaced by the fact that 'they' turned him into a church.

Alexandra quotes Francisco's line 'There's no one to bless you. And worse, there's no one to curse you' (*Plays: 3*, 156). This projects the play into Camus's absurd universe in which humanity's exile from sustaining wholeness is 'irremediable'. The conclusion she draws is that 'men [sic] are left to deal with their imperfection on their own, with no hope of forgiveness ...' I want to pick up on this with reference to an earlier moment where she points out, with regard to *The Morning After Optimism*, that 'The play echoes with the Christian rhetoric of good and evil, innocence and guilt ...' One thing which is striking with regard to Murphy's plays is

---

16   Fintan O'Toole, *The Politics of Magic* (Dublin: Raven Arts Press, 1987), p. 77.

the extent to which he does use Christian imagery: in *The Gigli Concert* we have references to Adam and, of course, the use of 'O Paradiso', in *Bailegangaire* we have Momo's reference to them as 'Poor banished children of Eve' (*Plays: 2*, 169) and in *Conversations on a Homecoming* there's Peggy's singing of 'All in the April Evening': 'All in the April Evening I thought on the lamb of God' (*Plays: 2*, 81). These two plays first point towards the restoration of a lost harmony – Anne in *Conversations* with her assertion that 'There's still the stream' and her final 'smiling her gentle hope out at the night' (*Plays: 2*, 87) – and its achievement in *Bailegangaire* with Mary's declaration that 'it was decided to give that – fambly of strangers another chance, and a brand new baby to gladden their home.' (*Plays: 2*, 170)

The use of religious imagery for radical – political – ends is a dominant feature of the writings of, particularly, members of the Frankfurt School who merged imagery of the Kabbala with Marxist analysis, the whole being directed to a re-demptive social transformation. To an extent we can perhaps say that Murphy is doing this in a modified form, using an available language of redemption and transformation in a poetically charged and suggestive way rather than actually advancing the philosophy – the theology – which originally underpinned that language. Alexandra identifies Francisco as 'an Irish Zarathustra' whose Nietzschean rhetoric 'subverts the very foundations of Christian morality'. The speech is interesting in this reversion as he looks forward to a day of judgement, the second coming, when 'Jesus, Man, total man, will call to his side the goats ... All those rakish, dissolute,

suicidal, fornicating goats … ' (*Plays: 3*, 155). Those who are
con-demned are the priests, they are 'blackguards', 'wretches'
who, as he says earlier, are the 'predators that have been mass-
produced out of the loneliness and isolation of people' (*Plays:
3*, 154). And while not abandoning the Nietzschean aspect of
the play – indeed of the plays – I'd want to include the
Nietzsche who, while advocating the critical history which
'judges and condemns' was equally concerned to stress that
this was not a call for cultural erasure with every generation.[17]
What he refers to as 'the plastic power' of a culture is only
valuable to the extent that it can 'assimilate and appropriate
the things of the past'. Indeed, on this capability depends the
'health of an individual, of a people and of a culture.' [18]
Murphy does, then, deconstruct Catholicism but I'm not sure
of the extent to which individuals now write their 'own texts
which recognize no allegiance to any preconceived dogma'.
Not that I disagree with Alexandra's formulation, rather I
question the absolute erasure this suggests. And I think we
can see a reconfiguration of the past specifically in *Bailegangaire*
and the fact that the new baby, like the dead grandson, is to be
called Tom.

The condition Murphy then identifies in these plays is, as I
said earlier, a condition of metaphysical desolation which is
exacerbated by social conditions and social constructions.

---

[17] Friedrich Nietzsche, 'On the uses and disadvantages of history
for life', in *Untimely Meditations*, trans. R. J. Hollingdale, introduction
J. P. Stern (Cambridge University Press, 1983), p. 72.

[18] *Ibid.*, pp. 62-3.

'Vital energy' Alexandra observes, 'can only spring from those who are excluded from prosperity and denied social recognition.' Here, in the issue of social exclusion, we have the critique of post-Treaty Ireland familiar from the writings of, for example, Sean Ó Faoláin through to the contemporary analysis of David Lloyd. But what I think is also the case in Murphy's work, in these two plays, is the urge for wholeness, forgiveness which is metaphysical; one in which, as in *Bailegangaire*, a future is predicated on the restoration of a baby to the 'fambly' or, as in *Sanctuary Lamp*, a resolution in which Harry's desired revenge on Francisco is replaced by a harmony signalled in Francisco's final, hesitant, 'We'll go together, right?' (*Plays: 3*, 160) and Harry's sleepy nod of agreement. Murphy's theatre is a secular theatre in its location, but I'd suggest it is profane in the original sense of *profanum*, outside the temple, but not disconnected from sacred concerns. I'm suggesting then that these plays have a religious, metaphysical dimension which is more than rhetorical.

In a recent article the Lacanian critic, Slavoj Žižek, asserted that 'the authentic Christian legacy is much too precious to be left to the fundamentalist freaks'.[19] For as Žižek reads Christianity it is profoundly social in that the key term is *agape*: literally a 'love feast' held by the early Christians in connection with the Lord's Supper but also, more loosely, applied to any Christian meal. It is, simply, an expression of brotherly love – and, also, I suggest, that image of the merging

---

[19] Slavoj Žižek, 'St. Paul: Or, The Christian Uncoupling', *The European English Messenger*, VIII:2 (Autumn 1999), 45.

of 'Loved Ones', the union for ever of loved ones with which
The Sanctuary Lamp closes. The argument Žižek advances is
that 'Through the Christian work of compassionate love' we
are able to accommodate what was disturbing and 'other' – as
perhaps Harry does with Francisco. And in a striking echo of
Murphy's plays Žižek emphasizes how Christ's teaching
suspended social order, accentuating 'those who belonged to
the very bottom of the social hierarchy the outcasts of society
(beggars, prostitutes …) as the privileged and exemplary
members of his new community. This new community is then
explicitly constructed as a collective of outcasts, the antipode
to any established … group.'[20] Here the Christian rhetoric
engages with what Alexandra refers to as the play's 'political
critique'. She's talking here about *The Morning After Optimism*
but it's equally true of *The Sanctuary Lamp*. While her specific
concerns are with political critique we are also in a world
which, while material, borders at least on the metaphysical. In
Žižek's terms 'love is work of love – the hard and arduous
work of repeated uncoupling, in which, again and again, we
have to disengage with the particular order we were born
into.'[21] Murphy's liminal locations, his marginal characters are
on one level outside the social order but, as the plays demonstrate, the struggle is to transcend its limitations. If the close
of *Morning After Optimism* is tentative, 'We done it, James' –
namely, found some liberation through the stabbing of
Edmund – we must note that '*They exit crying*' (*Plays: 3*, 96). In

---

20 *Ibid.*, 47.

21 *Ibid*, 49.

Sanctuary Lamp Harry's knifing of Francisco was the constant threat. The play closes, however, as they agree to 'go together' and Francisco's 'Good night, Har' and, after a pause, Harry's acknowledgement, 'Y' know' (*Plays: 3*, 160). We have, in other words, the triumph of *agape*, brotherly love, a concept which while Christian in origin is profoundly social in effect.

ill.6

ill.7

When she's gone he stands out of respect for her; his
like looks stunned, exhausted, frozen,
exhausted at her exhaustion.

Man   Thank you!

He gets a bottle of whisky.

Sc. 2.

Psychiatrist has entered.

Psychiatrist   Sit where you like Take a chair. Anywhere you like.

W—   I'll sit here then if you don't mind.

Psychiatrist   Well, I have your doctor's report here and —

Telephone rings.

Excuse me. Yes. Mrs. Reeves. Yes. No. Two. That's correct. No.
Two. That's correct. And Thursday week. (To the) Sorry
about that. Well, supposing you tell me the situation.

V—   Well, quite frankly, I don't know what I'm doing here.

Psy   Yes?

M—   Well, with all due respects I believe very little in
psychiatrists or social workers.

Psy   Why do you say Social workers?

M—   Oh, certainly, Social workers do very good work, excellent
work, work that's badly needed, I believe in them, but
not as applied to myself.

Psy   That were in the same field, I'm not a social worker.

M—   I know. What I meant to say was I believe very
little in Psychiatrists. I don't believe in them at all.
I'm not trying to be offensive.

Psy   I understand. How much do you drink.

M—   Well, lately, a little more than I did. Say, I can half
a litre of wine a night. And lately — if its of interest —
I've noticed myself gulping it, rather than — you know —
the usual sipping.

Psy   Do you ever drink more than a litre.

M—   I can remember one occasion doing so at home.
After had I suppose — though its hard to tell because

Talking it through: *The Gigli Concert, Bailegangaire*

Nicholas Grene

For someone who rings the Samaritans at 3 in the morning, for someone who lies back on the psychiatrist's couch, why should it help to talk about it? Is such talk an act of expression or of communication? Communication implies a two-way interchange, signals that go back and forth between talker and listener. Expression may travel just one way. The characters in Murphy's two great plays of the 1980s, *The Gigli Concert* and *Bailegangaire*, are traumatized, neurotic, or despairing creatures who feel compelled to talk, listen who will. Are they ever able actually to communicate with their interlocutors, or does their compulsive talking issue out of the self into a void? The action of both plays bears some resemblance to a psychotherapeutic process in which extreme emotional states are talked through towards healing. Does this then approximate to what Aristotle identified as the emotionally purgative effect of tragedy? What I am trying to come at in this pile-up of rhetorical questions is

how talk works in Murphy's plays: the relation between dialogue and overlapping monologues; the action of language in
the drama; what the characters say to one another and what
the plays say to the audience.

In a major essay published on *The Gigli Concert* last year,
Declan Kiberd reveals that Tom Murphy had been in analysis
with the psychiatrist Ivor Browne before he wrote the play.[22]
Even though it seems he discontinued the analysis, the play is
dedicated to Browne. In the mini-exhibition of manuscripts
we have mounted in the Long Room, you can see that at a
very early stage of writing the play, Murphy did draft scenes in
which the character who was to become the Irish Man
consults a perfectly ordinary psychiatrist. At that point, while
the notion for the play was still brewing, JPW King did not
exist as a character. By adding him in, but making the Man's
interlocutor not an orthodox clinical psychiatrist but a
'dynamatologist', Murphy in *The Gigli Concert* offers a deeply
ironic and subversive version of the patient-therapist
relationship.

JPW is, almost by his own admission, a quack, a charlatan.
The term 'dynamatologist' was apparently coined for Murphy
by Richard Kearney, for a philosopher of possibility, from the
Greek word 'dunamis', power or ability. From the beginning,
he is very evidently in as much need of help as his 'patient',
the Irish Man. (Of course, the Irish Man never gives his name,

---

[22] Declan Kiberd, 'Theatre as Opera: *The Gigli Concert*' in Eamonn
Jordan (ed.), *Theatre Stuff: Critical Essays on Contemporary Irish Theatre*
(Dublin: Carysfort Press, 2000), pp. 145-158.

but for convenience sake in this talk I am going to shorten him to just the Man.) The affinity between the two emerges early on when we hear the Man, without knowing, repeat the exact words spoken by JPW at the play's opening: 'Christ, how am I going to get through today?' (*Plays: 3*, 166, 173) In the patter that spills out from JPW under the shock of at last having a client, he is quite as confessional as the Man, in fact rather more so. When it comes to exploring sexual history it is JPW who has to reveal his 'first sexual encounter ... in mixed-infants' (*Plays: 3*, 214), to prompt the Man's hilarious re-collection of Maisie Kennedy trying to seduce him with sweets in the potato drills. Transference is of course a standard feature of the psychotherapeutic process in analysis, but it does not generally take the form of the analyst taking over the obsessions of his patient as JPW does. When JPW becomes crazily determined to sing like Gigli, just as the Man is cured of that mad desire, it is more like the passing of possession from one body to another.

JPW describes ironically what he calls the 'traditional' way of solving problems:

> I mean by sitting down together and playing the game called Slobs. The winner proves himself to be the most sentimental player and becomes King Slob by dealing, at the most unexpected moment, a sudden judas punch, or an emotional kick in the genitals to his opponent, thereby *getting* him. Problem solved. (*Plays: 3*, 199)

JPW and the Man do not exactly play Slobs through the action, but something like this confessional swap-session does go on, and it has the element of male competitiveness implicit in the confession game. It is the obsessiveness of specifically male egos that drives JPW and the Man's tendency to talk at one another, past one another. This is brought out by the figure of Mona. Some critics have wondered whether Mona is really necessary in the play, given how relatively small a part she has. (Murphy did write her out of a two-hander radio version of the play.) Declan Kiberd has argued persuasively, in the essay I have already mentioned, that Mona is in fact crucial as the feminine principle that both the men repress. If we accept that, then the very fact that she is sidelined is significant in itself. 'You're not listening to me' (*Plays: 3*, 190), is Mona's first line in Scene Four, and it is her theme tune. JPW, locked in his growing obsession with the Man's obsession, in his infatuation with his unseen telephonic Helen, cannot relate to the woman who is in bed with him, cannot relate to her, that is, until it is too late when she has been diagnosed as having terminal cancer.

Murphy casts a cold eye at the wrestling match of talk that goes on between his two male characters in so far as it resembles a patient/analyst relationship. But he also calls in question the forms of narrative with which identity itself is made up in language. When JPW tries to get the Man to tell him his life story, what he gets is a sort of verbal karaoke, as the Irish Man mimes to Gigli's autobiography:

IRISH MAN. I was born with a voice and little else.

JPW. Naked we came into the world.

IRISH MAN. We were very poor.

JPW. What did your father do?

IRISH MAN. A cobbler.

JPW. Making or mending them? It could be significant.

IRISH MAN. He started by making them but factory-made shoes soon put paid to that.

JPW. Where was this?

IRISH MAN. Recanati.

JPW. Recan?

IRISH MAN. Ati.

JPW. What county is that in?

IRISH MAN. Recanati is in Italy. (*Plays: 3*, 176)

In this first version, the Man is Benamillo, his elder brother Abramo; later his elder brother will be Hibernicized back into Mick, a tyrannical elder brother in one reminiscence of childhood, a saintly and protective elder brother in a second. Murphy does more here than demonstrate the fictiveness of memory; he exposes the generic stereotyping of the telling of the life. This is most evident in the counterpart stories of unattainable romantic passion that the two men trade. There was Ida, the telephone operator whom the Man in his Gigli incarnation adored from afar, and who died of a broken heart because denied his love by cruel, class-conscious parents. JPW can easily see this as the corny fantasy it is. But he is most indignant when the Man points out the similarity between that story and JPW's mad passion for the unobtainable Helen: 'My

story is about a real live living person, your story is bullshit'
(*Plays: 3*, 210). But of course we in the audience can see that
they are both bullshit, both the kind of dramatic fiction with
which men fantasize their lives.

I have been talking so far throughout as if *The Gigli Concert*
is entirely composed of talk. It isn't: it is a concert as well as a
play. When we aren't listening to the two men talk, even for a
great deal of the time when we are, we are also listening to
Gigli sing. The Man's very opening words, even before he
enters are 'Can I come in? … To talk … To sing' (*Plays: 3*,
166). 'Like you can talk forever' he says later, 'but singing.
Singing, d'yeh know? The only possible way to tell people …
Who you are?' (*Plays: 3*, 23) To be set against this is JPW's
answer to Mona at the start of the play's last scene as they lie
in bed together listening to Gigli:

> MONA. What's he singing, what's he saying now?
>
> JPW. You don't have to know, whatever you like.
>
> MONA. Beloved.
>
> JPW. If you like. (*Plays: 3*, 231)

(I find it very interesting that this piece of dialogue appears
already in the earliest stage of conception of the play, represented in that notebook on display in the Long Room,
when it was the Man – Benamillo to be – who is apparently
having the affair with Mona: her character, not that of JPW,
was there from the start.) The Man's obsessive desire to sing
like Gigli is a desire for the transcendent form of expression
that, in music as against mere talk, allows you truly to 'tell

people ... who you are'. Yet by the end the expressiveness of singing does not have to be located as the expression of any one identity or meaning. It can be appropriated to the mood and feeling of the listener. What can be the significance of Gigli singing operatic arias in unintelligible Italian, arias from nineteenth-century operas with situations more wildly melo-dramatic and absurd than JPW's romance over Helen, the Man's sob story of Ida?

You could, if you wanted, take *The Gigli Concert* as a nice illustration of Walter Benjamin's famous essay on 'The Work of Art in the Age of Mechanical Reproduction'.[23] Benjamin, you remember, argues that in a modern age where works of art can be reproduced by photograph, on film, by gramo-phones (as they were in Benjamin's time), what disappears is the cult of authenticity vested in the idea of an original. The ritual associations of the work when it was unique and de-livered only within a specific context are eroded and event-ually destroyed when it can be endlessly reproduced and 'performed' at will in public or in private. *The Gigli Concert* brilliantly enacts that proposition. What we hear in the theatre – heard last night in the Abbey – were recordings made of a long dead Italian tenor, sounds recorded with one sort of technology and then mediated by other forms of technology. We watch the fictional characters of JPW and the Man, created by Tom Murphy, as they listen to these artificially reproduced sounds. When Mark Lambert as JPW 'sings' Gigli

---

23 Walter Benjamin, *Illuminations*, trans. Harry Zohn (London: Fontana, 1973), pp. 211-235.

at the end, we know that he is miming to the record. Most
striking of all perhaps, as a symbol of Benjamin's essay, is the
final theatrical image of Gigli on endless repeat singing out to
the abandoned and empty stage-set.

You could take this one stage further to a full postmodernist reading of the play. In this view, *The Gigli Concert*
would be interpreted as an assertion that there is no such
thing as an authentic self, or the possibility of self-expression.
There are only modes and forms of discourse any one of
which can be mimed or mimicked, none of them capable of
telling it like it is, because there is no such thing as a verifiable
mode of being to tell it like. To me the puzzle of the play is to
say why that is *not* its effect, why at the end it should feel to us
in the theatre as though something <u>had</u> been talked through,
something *had* been expressed. It is partly because the theatrical moment of JPW singing like Gigli is a bravura performance, the consummation towards which the whole action has
been driving, even though we do of course know it is only an
actor miming it. It constitutes a kind of miracle, as does JPW's
survival of all the drink and drugs he has taken to enable him
to do it. His exit at the end feels like a triumph; he has come
through. But there is also the fact that we are hearing Gigli's
singing and even if it is a mechanically reproduced recording
of sounds made long ago, it still has the power to express, and
even to communicate as high art. I have been playing around
with the idea of *The Gigli Concert* as a modernist, even a
postmodernist text. Let me suggest instead that the feeling of
the play is that of a postromantic romanticism. For all its
ironies, its self-conscious awareness of role-playing, and the

mimicry of language and voices, Murphy remains a Romantic writer in his conception of an art driven by emotional extremities, and in his claims for the expressive value and meaning of such an art.

If *The Gigli Concert* might be used to illustrate one famous essay of Benjamin, *Bailegangaire* could be linked to another equally famous, called 'The Storyteller'. In that piece Benjamin sees the storyteller as an archaic figure in the modern world, a modernity that 'has quite gradually removed narrative from the realm of living speech',[24] replacing experience, mediated in the oral forms of story, with information processed in print and other technological media. What could better dramatize this idea than the figure of the aged shanachie Mommo, sitting up in the bed telling out her story, while Dolly comes in from a 1980s Ireland with the helicopters circling overhead and the Japanese deciding whether to shut down the computer plant down the road. The two plays, *The Gigli Concert* and *Bailegangaire* could be seen as complementary opposites, the one illustrating the art of grand opera in an age of mechanical reproduction, the other the traditional folk form of storytelling as it lingers on in an only belatedly modernizing Ireland.

I was very taken with this idea when it first occurred to me, the notion of the two plays so neatly relating to the two essays of Benjamin – and it's astonishing how far-seeing those essays, written back in 1936, still seem. But then I became

---

[24] *Ibid.* p. 86.

uneasy with that neatness. It is partly because of the sardonic treatment Murphy gives to the motif of storytelling in *Bailegangaire*. For Benjamin, storytelling is the way in which the experience of generations is stored and transmitted. 'The cardinal point for the unaffected listener', he says, 'is to assure himself of the possibility of reproducing the story. Memory is the epic faculty *par excellence* ... Memory creates the chain of tradition which passes a happening on from generation to generation'.[25] For Benjamin this is a beneficent phenomenon, but in Murphy's play it is one that has broken down, has become dysfunctional. Mary and Dolly, the grown-up grand-daughters who have endlessly had to listen to Mommo's endless story do not want to remember it, they want to forget it. As Mary says bitterly when Dolly offers to buy her a video, 'I have a video here already' (*Plays: 2*, 142). Mommo's story telling too is art in an age of mechanical reproduction. It is constantly re-played; it can be stopped and started, almost at will by a prompt from Mary or Dolly. Each of them knows the story so by heart that they can take over the recitation of it as an exercise in ironic mimicry. Benjamin's model of story telling as the transmission of experience from generation to generation has been emptied of meaning in the spectacle of the senile Mommo telling the tale of the laughing-contest in the presence of her alienated granddaughters.

The three women that we see on stage in *Bailegangaire* are all three locked into dead-end compulsions; the capacity for communication is blocked for each of them. Mommo tells out

---

[25] *Ibid*, p. 96-7.

her story to the imagined small grandchildren at the end of her bed, but that storytelling is in some sense a deliberate blocking out of her real grown-up granddaughter Mary and her need for recognition. According to the stage directions, she watches 'MARY *and* MARY*'s movements suspiciously*', as she says 'An' no one will stop me! Tellin' my nice story ...' (*Plays: 2*, 92). The condition of senile dementia is, almost by definition, that of imprisonment within the self, the inability to connect with a world without. But in the case of Mommo there is also a sense of the wilful shutting out of attempts to reach her. Mary in the anguish of her loneliness and isolation needs just that recognition which Mommo denies her, the recognition that might allow her to feel that she belongs. Yet in her relationship with her sister Dolly there is that fraught sibling hostility that can only insist on her own grievance against the other. They have been defined in that crudest of polarities, Mary has the brains, Dolly the looks, and they each resent the other one's attributes. For Mary her sister is 'that bitch Dolly', with her irresponsible promiscuity; for Dolly, Mary is the stuck-up educated sister who managed to get away – 'You had it easy'.

In *The Gigli Concert* Murphy may have exposed a specifically male phallocentrism, the male egotism of the word. But in *Bailegangaire* he showed himself wary of what has sometimes become a sentimental feminist alternative: a female model of mutual openness and solidarity, successive generat-ions of women as a benign image of matriarchal descent. The terrible, vengeful, destructive Mommo is the old sow who eats her farrow in person. The strange utterance that she repeats so

often – 'Och hona ho gus hah-haa' – Murphy has explained is
not a lament, related to the Irish 'Ochón', but a cry of
triumph. The concluding chord in her vivid, frightening
grotesque evocation of the chorus of laughter at the catalogue
of misfortunes is 'The nicest night ever' (*Plays: 2*, 165). Still, at
whatever distance in time it may be since the events of that
night, the fierce vindictiveness against the Bochtáns – the
'jolter-headed gobshites' – has not abated. The energies of
Bailegangaire are again and again the energies of hatred that can
find no adequate outlet. It is after Dolly has left that Mary
shouts out the secret of her affair with Dolly's husband
Stephen: 'Your husband wined and dined and bedded me!
(*Realizing she has been talking to the door*) I'm going soft in the
head' (*Plays: 2*, 113). Dolly's appallingly vivid aria of hate
against men in the second act cannot be simply exorcized by
falling drunkenly asleep in the family bed with her sister and
grandmother.

Murphy resists easy resolutions to the desperate situation
of the women in *Bailegangaire*, a situation that is the more
desperate because it is one they share but can apparently only
experience alone. What gradually comes to work against that
sense of locked-in, locked-out isolation of the characters from
one another, is the musical relationship of the voices in the act
of expressiveness which is the play itself. This is something I
cannot begin to illustrate in this paper, but just listen to it as
we watch the performance tonight. Listen to the way in which
a disjointed phrase like 'the cursed paraffin' is sounded early
on and reappears several times before its meaning within the
story becomes clear. Listen to the way Mary and Dolly's com-

ments from outside Mommo's narrative echo and counter-point its continuing melody. And after Mary determines to egg Mommo on to finish the story, we begin to get not dialogue but duologue and eventually duet between them, as they come to sing together. The harmonies that emerge out of the dissonant voices of Mommo, Mary and Dolly are heard harmonies for us in the audience rather than the shared harmony of communication between the three of them.

And yet, of course, by the end of the play, there is also to some degree that other harmony in the characters' relationship as well. It is there when Mary repeats to Dolly the words spoken to her by her terminally ill patient years before, 'You're going to be alright, Mary', which she has carried around for years 'Like, a *promised* blessing' (*Plays: 2*, 160). When Mary says 'You're going to be alright, Dolly' (*Plays: 2*, 167), it is as though she is able to pass on that blessing; it is perhaps the moment at which she decides to accept Dolly's baby. Most movingly there is the final recognition accorded to Mary when Mommo at last speaks her name: 'And sure a tear isn't such a bad thing, Mary, and haven't we everything we need here, the two of us' (*Plays: 2*, 169). The ending of Mommo's story is of course the event around which these gestures of reconciliation cluster. By bringing the story to an end it is possible to bridge the gap in communication between the characters as it is also a generation gap. In making the granddaughters Mary and Dolly adult women, Murphy pushes the action of the laughing-contest right back in time, almost out of history altogether. There was an earlier stage at which he worked out a quite tight, quite specific chronology: you may have seen it illustrated in our exhibition. What he brought out in the final version of the play is the disjunction between the archaic world of Mommo's story telling and the – at the time of writing – absolutely contemporary world of Mary and Dolly in 1984. When the story of the laughing-contest is brought to an end, when its tragic consequences in the early childhood lives of Mary and Dolly are brought to light, connections are made allowing the lost generations of the dead and the trauma of their loss to be acknowledged.

These two plays are counterparts to one another in their play with the issues of expressiveness with which I started. They illustrate together the extraordinary range and reach of Murphy's theatrical imagination. It is as at home with the placeless, displaced space in which *The Gigli Concert* is played out – presumably Dublin but it never explicitly says so – as in the familiar country cottage of *Bailegangaire*. He can work as effectively with the idiom of European operatic singing, demystified in an age of mechanical reproduction, as with the archaic Irish oral art of the shanachie. The difference between the two is the degree to which what is felt to be expressed by the end of *Bailegangaire* is the experience of a collectivity, a community. The characters of *The Gigli Concert* are typical of modernist art in their complete disjunction from one another; they are strangers who have no necessary connection with one another, the shards of their experience arbitrarily juxtaposed. In *The Gigli Concert* it is out of that disjunctive juxtaposition that artistic meaning is made. It is Romantic only in the defiant confidence of its belief in the possibility of full mean-ing in full artistic expressiveness. In *Bailegangaire*, unlike in *The*

Gigli Concert, the characters are bound together in the inextricable knots of family dynamics. But by recuperating the history of that family in all its psychic deformations, in forcing through the mythic story of the laughing-contest to its end, the play enacts a sort of family therapy that expresses the trauma of a nation for all of us who share in it.

ill.9

Response

Declan Kiberd

When, at the end of *The Gigli Concert*, we hear the sublime voice of Gigli captured in a flawed, scratchy phonograph record, we know that one of Murphy's obsessions is the expression of true feeling through flawed media. The feeling is always authentic, positive, assured – the problem is that the forms into which it is poured never seem quite right. Often they seem to humiliate rather than embody the intended emotion.

I think that Nicky had made a very useful distinction between communciation and expression in that context. A great deal of what masquerades as dialogue in Murphy, as in Beckett, is actually an exercise of competing monologues, engaged in by those who, like Beckett's characters, have little to say but everything to express, as they go in search of some form that might accommodate their mess.

Music is a perfect embodiment of the issue, because it is more often expression – making no insistence on an immediate vocal response. Even stories can seem to seek some sort of comment – as when the two men, Irish Man and JPW become annoyed at how flawed the image of the ideal woman at the other end of a phone-line actually is: 'My story is about a real life living person, your story is bullshit'. Where I'd disagree with Nicky is when he says that both are bullshit male fantasies. I'd prefer to see them as perfected emotions which have sought expression through a flawed and inappropriate medium. It is as if the two men, on hearing the Gigli record, are noticing and arguing about the scratches, rather than permitting the sublime singing to override them.

Every form attempted is an experiment, a try-out for size on the part of the available feeling – and some will be found to fit better than others, as in an adolescent trying out roles. The extreme male competitiveness between the two adults has something of an adolescent quality about it – but I don't think this means they are lacking in a sense of self. JPW at the end may imitate Gigli – in an act of inspired imitation – but this is not karaoke at the finish: the disconnected plug proves that he had indeed grown into the pose and made it his own. This is of course an ancient aesthetic principle of the Abbey Theatre – based on the Yeatsian notion of an anti-self, 'of all things not impossible the most difficult', with which a person might fuse, his own seeming opposite revealed as secret double. It is the wisdom of 'one that ruffled in a manly pose/ For all his timid heart' or of Synge's Christy becoming a mighty man by the power of a lie. But the point is that JPW really does sing like Gigli – that Christy really did win all at the sports – that these moments of greatness, when the actual and the symbolic fuse, are rare but real enough, and made possible if people are brave and intrepid enough to do what Yeats wanted – to copy the ideal image held out by art.

And part of the wisdom of the play is its revelation that art is truly achieved in those moments when the self embraces the flawed but beautiful medium, and allows itself to be chastened by it – as a sculptor is educated by the stone which nonetheless he seeks to master and to put into a different shape. The resistance of the medium to absolute shaping adds to our sense of pleasure in the final achievement – there is always a silent reference of ideal artistic works back to actual human abilities. To seek absolute mastery of the medium, to want it absolutely perfect, would be in fact to abort the necessary dialectic between feeling and form – and to produce not art at all but a merely repressive analysis. The play is, among other things, a brilliant satire not only on the rather reductive analysis of personal crises provided by most modern psychotherapy, but also on those modes of literary expression which seek to tame rather than unleash the energies latent in a medium. The true work of art is always in that sense too late for logic.

This doesn't, it seems to me, have to lead to a postmodern indifferentism – to a perception that there may be no authentic self and no possibility of expression. Forms of discourse do indeed precede us to those experiences which we expect to be the most searingly personal moments of our lives – but those forms are not simply mimicked or mimed. An

imitation of an action, as the classic authors knew, is itself a
new action. To make the Gigli sound in 1983 may not be at all
the same experience as to have made it in 1927; and anyhow
no two sounds could ever be quite alike. True originality, in
fact, is far more likely to come to those who have the courage
to rely on tradition and to allow it flow through them. The
Ireland of 1983 was filled with designer-Stalinists who kept
telling us to create *ex nihilo* – as if there were no preceding
voices – and look how derivative they now sound compared
with people like Murphy and Friel who allowed the past flow
through them.

Nicky has made a lot of the notion of the gramophone-
player as a machine confronting a work of art in the age of
mechanical reproduction. He says that this means that what
disappears is the cult of authenticity vested in the idea of an
original. But I wonder. After all, Walter Benjamin saw the dis-
integration of ancient aura as an inherently desirable thing,
part of that process of modern democracy which divested
artworks of their distance and their sense of existing in a
privileged space. Rather than see JPW as an abject karaoke
illustration of John Stuart Mill's idea that freedom in the
modern world has turned out to be the freedom to be just like
everyone else, we should, I think, see the final moments as a
celebration of the healing power of art (over analysis) and also
as a celebration of the ordinary man as potential artist. This is
not the modern triumph of the analytic therapist but of the
artist-therapist. For JPW is also a form, a medium – and the
music has called forth from him an energy that is always
latent, or at least long dormant and unused in himself.

Such an energy always exists just a millimetre or two on this side of madness – a process recognized and explored in *Bailegangaire* – but part of the point there is that there must be a true dialectic, a real exchange, if ancient narrative is not to lapse into autism. The scene thus created has often struck me as a mimic version of *Riders to the Sea*, in which two adult daughters manage not to hear or else to mishear the complaints of an old woman with one thing and she saying it over.

It is not just romantic of Murphy to believe in the possibility of art as transcendence: it is Utopian. And it is based on the notion of energies available to us from the past which cry out for redemption and use in the present. Where there is a real engagement, a transmission, all is well, provided that the receiver is working as hard as the transmitter. In *The Gigli Concert* an atom that seemed destined to spark off a new energy with another atom finally collided fruitfully with another, releasing the beautiful new pulses that make a future possible: but in *Bailegangaire*, as Nicky said, the very idea of the transmissibility of culture is thrown into sharp question. For these reasons, I would therefore see both plays as more different than Nicky suggested – the earlier one holding out a hope that in the latter seems just not possible.

PART TWO: TALKING TO TOM MURPHY

Tom Murphy |
In Conversation with Michael Billington

Abbey Theatre, 7 October 2001

MB   *It's a great pleasure to be sitting here talking to Tom Murphy on this occasion: it is wonderful to have a season of this kind to celebrate an illustrious living dramatist, a season that shows the diversity and range of the work. Tom, can we begin by talking about this season and its significance: the first obvious question is how did it arise? Did you one day get a call from Ben Barnes saying should we do a season? Did it involve any discussion? How did it actually start?*

TM   Well, I got the phone call from Ben which left me in suspense because he didn't say why he wanted to come to see me, and when he did, he said he would like to do a season which surprised me greatly. And it went on from there.

MB   *How was the season built up? You must have had a very strong hand in the selection of the plays.*

TM   As far as I remember, I left it to Ben to do the preliminary lists, and he did a number of permutations on lists that could be done. Then we met and discussed the different plays and added here, subtracted there. The season brings me up to 1985. *The House* and *The Wake* had been done so recently that it made sense to look for punctuation marks prior to the recent plays.

MB   *You said a moment ago it surprised you. Why did it surprise you, when Ben proposed the season?*

TM   One doesn't expect such an honour. It is an incredible honour that the artistic director of our national theatre and the people working here should consider the plays worthy of a season. That said, acknowledging that I am honoured, I have found it very strange. The type of play I write, including those selected for this season, seeks for some kind of emotion – a pure emotion or as close to purity as I can achieve. The season has been very strange in that I have not just been revisiting the plays, I have been on a journey backwards in my own life. The plays often start from a personal mood, and as they progress I try to get deeper and deeper into that mood until it transcends the autobiographical and hopefully I find a mood that is recognizably universal. It has sometimes been said by my nearest and dearest that I have tempted sanity by this digging deep into emotions, particularly the emotions that are to do with depression. Seeing the plays over the last week, and seeing them so well done and so realized and made incarnate, has been very strange in the way they have churned things up in me. I'm proud that they are being done, but if this season brings me up to 1985, I'm not suggesting to Ben

Barnes that he should already be thinking of 1985 to 2002 because I think I would need quite a long breather before another one should happen.

MB   *I'd like to come on to the specific sources of some of the plays as we carry on talking. But can we first go back to the beginning and the shaping influences on your work? I'm intrigued by your early life in Tuam: a small town, I take it therefore fairly restrictive and repressive. Was theatre for you from the beginning an escape route from the circumstances of your upbringing?*

TM   Yes and no. There wasn't that much theatre. There was always an amateur theatre group that dated back to before 1900, and in my childhood my mother took me to see a number of plays in the Town Hall done by the local group; then I saw Anew McMaster on a few occasions visiting Tuam. In my earliest experiences of watching theatre – and of cinema – it was the attentive reverent silence of the audience that impressed me as much as what was happening on the stage.

MB   *I know that you worked in amateur theatre, acted and directed plays in Tuam. Do you think that acting in plays is an essential preparation for any incipient dramatist teaching you about the rhythm of dialogue and the structure of a scene?*

TM   I'm sure. I'd be very clear on the fact that the kind of acting I was doing convinced me that my future didn't lie in acting. But no matter what one does, the actual practical business of treading the boards, absorbing other people's plays, not necessarily consciously but recognizing instinctively that they have got rhythms and there is contrast, there is development of plot, there is evolution of character and so on, is invaluable.

MB   *You imply you weren't a wonderful actor. Are you being mock modest? How good were you?*

TM   I am being mock modest.

MB   *I read that amongst the dramatists you admired from early on were Lorca and Tennessee Williams. Was that because of their qualities of poetry, sexuality and an escape from a restrictive kitchen realism? Was it because of the otherness that they represented?*

TM   I'd say yes, otherness. Perhaps it was even more indicative of the type of life that I felt myself in where anything Irish was a pain in the arse. And that included O'Casey and Synge. It was a stultifying time; it wasn't just my home town, the culture that pervaded the whole country was repressive. We were very insular – we congratulated ourselves on our insularity – that was part of the ideology that prevailed. I felt anything Irish couldn't be good, and so peculiarly I had to find Synge through Lorca, Lorca who was of course greatly influenced by Synge, and it was ten or fifteen years later after my first sortie into writing with my old friend Noel O'Donoghue that I realized and boggled and knelt before the genius of O'Casey. Lorca's poetic form of drama appealed to me greatly, as did Tennessee Williams. I confess I was alerted to the fact that a play called *A Streetcar Named Desire* existed because a film of the play came to my home town and everybody – certainly the Legion of Mary or Children of Mary – were told not to attend it on pain of expulsion, and one of my sisters was one of six girls from the town who defied the edict from the church. A few years later I came across *A Streetcar* on a barrow outside a bookshop. At that time I didn't see the play as being about Blanche at all but about Stanley: the line of least resistance for me was to see solely how the male character behaved. Williams's dialogue was the most naturalistic I had encountered. I had read a bit of Chekhov, Strindberg and so on, but they were chalk marks on the wall: I've read that, I've read that. But Williams – the energy of Williams and what I thought was his naturalism which is of course lyricism – was a great punctuation mark in my life: to read this dialogue as against the translated Chekhov, the translated Ibsen, Strindberg.

MB　*That brings us to your first full-length play. I know you had written before that but* A Whistle in the Dark, *the very set of which we sit on now here in the Abbey, was your first fully-fledged independent play. Having seen it again last night, I have a lot of questions I'd love to ask. The first one is about how close it was to your own circumstances. I don't mean literally in so far as you were still living in Tuam but your father had already gone to work in England, and your brothers had also migrated to England. Was this the starting point for the play, the sense of a family diaspora that was going on? Did that trigger the idea for the play in your mind?*

TM　It's forty years this year since the play was produced, and I now wonder who the man was who wrote it. I'm astonished at how extraordinarily well structured the play is. I wish I could now structure a play as well as *Whistle in the Dark*. What you say is true about how my personal life was influenced by emigration. When I started to go to England, usually for the summer months, whether to work on the buses or on the buildings or in pubs, I of course gravitated to places where my brothers were including areas which had become pre-dominantly Irish ghettos. There was an extraordinary cult of violence in those places that I still don't understand. Some of the reasons for the violence were that the men had money for perhaps the first time in their lives, and they did drink too; but much more importantly perhaps, they had a sense of being betrayed by the country of their origin here, and they also felt that they had betrayed that country. They were carrying a most curious guilt that they were very much inferior to the people they had left behind, and they were people who didn't belong in England. When they came back for the summer sojourn, they found they didn't quite belong here either. Strange dichotomies had grown up in them, and they didn't know what to do with themselves, with their freedom, with their money, with this fragmented, fractured identity. All that I observed, or absorbed rather than observed. A brother of mine had told me a very cruel and awful story about a family that operated around the Birmingham area, in which one of them carried half of another man's ear in a match box. I was shocked, amazed, fascinated even by this – the cannibalism, the primitiveness of it – and I think that this story became a triggering action to set about a play that was waiting within me to be written. The play achieved a degree of notoriety because somebody breaks a bottle over another person's head onstage, but I think it is more about the emotionally charged blood knot that is the family, that is every family.

MB   *Every family, you say: is it not a peculiarly Irish condition that you're dealing with in this play?*

TM   I don't think it is. As I say, it is forty years since it was done first: if anything, it's attracting bigger audiences now wherever it's played. When it was first done, women were terrified of that play; when it was done the time before this time – I think it was 1988 or 89 – of the 100 people who came up to me to say well done I'd say 96 of them were women. They had started to identify with the play in some fashion.

MB   *You said quite rightly that it is an extremely well structured play, a perfectly proportioned play. Watching it again last night, I was struck by something else: it has a very interesting moral ambivalence. One of the key speeches comes towards the end when Harry talks to his brother Michael about the way he's always been patronized by Michael; Michael has always explained, everyone has always explained everything to him. Without in any way condoning or endorsing Harry's values, you seem there to be expressing an extraordinary sympathy and understanding for that character and the culture from which he springs; in other words, it is not simply a play which is about the evils of violence, it's a play that's understanding the roots and the sources of violence within us. Is that fair and accurate?*

TM   That's very fair and accurate. I'm a great admirer, as I've said, of Tennessee Williams; I also admire Arthur Miller but for different reasons. Where I would disagree with Miller is in his tendency to moralize; it was once said that the failure of the moralist is the triumph of the tragedian. In *Whistle in the Dark*, as you point out, I'm not passing judgements on these people. I found that I was greatly sympathetic towards the character of Harry. Michael may be the principal character in the play, but in certain ways Harry is like the hidden hero who is articulating for the thick people of the world.

MB   *As you say it's not a moralistic play. How much, though, did you put yourself into the play, your own personal self. Is there something of you in Michael?*

TM   I think there is something of all the characters, something in all the characters of me. I know that when I wrote it I had a feeling that I was spreading myself out among the characters. People I had met and absorbed too were feeding the evolution of the characters to make them something fuller, more than just aspects of myself. But in the character of the father I felt totally at sea. I thought that this character was completely incredible, and yet he is the one that most people talk about as having known.

MB   *You mean that kind of man with that type of bravura and bluster?*

TM   Yes. You can look on Dada as some kind of Hitler figure who creates an army to deal with his own impotence, his own failure, his own shallowness, his own inability to cope with life, or you can take the lesser figures of fathers or uncles that we may have had, that we watched in action.

MB   *It's interesting the influence this play may or may not have had on other writers. You wrote that play in 1960 and Harold Pinter's* The Homecoming *came along five years later. Do you recognize similarities between Pinter's play and yours or not?*

TM   I do, yes.

MB   *Does Harold?*

TM   He's never mentioned it to me.

MB   *Did he see your play?*

TM   I believe he did. Nobody has the copyright on an idea, it depends on how far one takes the idea. I've been influenced by O'Casey, Synge, Arthur Miller, Tennessee Williams, by figures such as Big Daddy or James Tyrone or the family situations in their plays. We are all influenced; we all influence each other.

MB   *Yes, I'm not suggesting that Pinter's play is in any way a plagiaristic version of yours, I'm just saying that it's very interesting that he comes up with the same family structure. Famously* A Whistle in the Dark *was done at Stratford East and was rejected by the theatre we are now sitting in. Did that influence your decision to go and live in London, the fact that* Whistle in the Dark *had been taken by Joan Littlewood and was then done in the West End? Was that one of the reasons you went to London?*

TM   Incidentally, this is a recurring error that Joan Littlewood was involved.

MB   *She was not?*

TM   She wasn't: it was immediately after her tenure at the Theatre Royal. But undoubtedly if Ernest Blythe had accepted the play for the Abbey I possibly would not have emigrated. I think it was fortunate for me that he did not, and that I could spend the decade of the sixties in London to shed some of the insularity that I talked about, to become more objective. Geographically removed from one's own country there is a type of objectivity that one achieves, and I certainly would not have achieved that objectivity, my vision would have been constricted had I stayed here. I had that privilege of being in

London to learn my trade, to watch world theatre over there: the great Peter Daubeney seasons where one saw the national theatre of Greece, one saw Ingmar Bergman's *Hedda Gabler*, the National Theatre then playing at the old Vic, the wonderful work that was happening at the Royal Court – I was exposed to all that.

MB   *Yes, it so happens that the last fortnight I've seen five or six plays of the 1960s including your own, and one suddenly realizes what a fantastic decade that was for theatre everywhere. I'm very interested in the time you spent in London in the sixties. You said it gave you greater objectivity, a distance from Ireland, and yet at the same time much of the work that you wrote in London during that decade was about Ireland, about Irish history. You wrote* Famine *in that period, you wrote* The Patriot Game *dealing with 1916 during that period: were you able to look at Irish history more clearly because you were actually not living in Ireland?*

TM   I think so. We're back to objectivity. *Famine* emerged from my reading of Cecil Woodham-Smith's *The Great Hunger* which was quite an event in the publishing world in 1962 or 63. I was bowled over by the book – I thought there would be several plays written on the subject of the Irish Famine. Nothing happened. So after two years I started to do my own research on it and, as I researched the famine in Ireland, I looked further afield to Europe to what was going on there in the mid-nineteenth century. Ireland was by no means the only country stricken with famine in those days. I came across a book about a famine among the Eskimos written by a French man, and in translation it also was called *The Great Hunger*. I was reading magazines and newspapers about what was happening in Bihar to get the contemporary scene. I don't know that I would have been doing that had I stayed on in Ireland. I found then that when I started the actual writing, I came to wonder was I a student of famine or a victim? It didn't make sense to me to write a play about an historical event, no matter how major an event: that would appear to be a gratuitous thing. So I began to think of what I call my own time, say the mid-20th century, the 1950s, and thinking about the culture that I grew up in, how repressed, how harsh I thought Irish womanhood was. How the natural extravagance of youth, young manhood, young womanhood, was repressed, while the people preaching messages of meekness, obedience, self-control I observed had mouths that were bitter and twisted. And I began to feel that perhaps the idea of food, the absence of food, is only one element of famine: that all of those other poverties attend famine, that people become silent and secretive, intelligence becomes cunning. I felt that the hangover of the 19th century famine was still there in my time; I felt that the Irish mentality had become twisted.

MB   *That's a very powerful statement. In the Introduction to the Methuen published text of* Famine, *you say something very extra-ordinary to me: you say you have no politics. This may be irony because you go on partly to disclaim it; but the statement you've just made about the way famine permeates a culture and survives its own time – that is a political statement. When you say that you have no politics in that Introduction to* Famine, *are you being deliberately ironical? Presumably you do have strong convictions?*

TM   Yes, I do, but I'm not being ironical. The danger in saying that one is politically minded is that a commentator, an academic, a critic will come along and seek solely the political line in the play, with the result that the play is reduced to the linear line that is its political attitude. In the kind of writing that I try to achieve, politics is only one aspect of the tapestry. I've mentioned the emotional aspect of things, the folly, the wisdom of characters. In my time as a writer it is only recently that people have begun to accept that my work starts from emotions and moods, emotions and moods that may be difficult to comment on or to write about. Of course I am politically minded but it is not at the top of my agenda; it is part of the tapestry that is woven.

MB *When you say you have no politics, what you seem to be saying is that you distrust the labelling that politics brings not the politics themselves, is that right? You don't want to be categorized as a writer?*

TM It isn't to do with categorization. Think of Chekhov and the tapestry that he weaves; one is conscious that there is a huge political movement happening behind but one isn't thinking about that when one sees or reads Chekhov. Similarly with Shakespeare: there is an enormous amount of politics and history of course in Shakespeare, his characters are kings and so on, but were he writing today he might achieve an equivalent complexity by taking his extremes from a different walk of life.

MB *Are you a person of very strong political convictions in the private arena, in your private life, I mean away from writing for the stage? Are you a man for whom politics matters?*

TM   No, I'm not. I wouldn't be running out every day to buy *The Irish Times* – or *The Guardian*. But I think that any sensible fair-minded person is a socialist.

MB   *That's a fairly political statement, isn't it?*

TM   Well, what is socialism if not equity, fair play for people; if the word socialism didn't exist, we wouldn't even be thinking of inventing it: fair-minded people would be thinking along the lines of the great socialists.

MB   *If we follow on the narrative of your life and career, the 1970s were very productive for you and two of the plays from that time are included in the Abbey season. But I read that in the late 1970s you for a period gave up writing and took up gardening. Is that a literal truth?*

TM   Yes.

MB   *Why did you give up writing?*

TM   Well, I had acquired a garden and the previous play that I had written – serious play that I had written – was *The Sanctuary Lamp*, and I certainly didn't want to let myself in for an experience like that again. I also had the naïve belief that it might be possible to be happy in a garden, and after two years of gardening I found out that you couldn't be happy in a garden.

MB   *So Voltaire was wrong.*

TM   He was; and if you cannot be happy in a garden, you cannot be happy anywhere, so hence you become quite happy about it, having resolved the matter.

MB   *I'm still intrigued by the gardening: was it purely therapeutic and recreational, or were you actually market gardening and selling produce?*

TM   Well, the plan was to be a market gardener. In fact, I was going to specialize in rhododendrons and heathers.

MB   *But you didn't carry on with this?*

TM   I didn't. No, I discovered that one needed a great amount of bottom heat to grow rhododendrons.

MB   *Right, and you didn't have the bottom heat?*

TM   I didn't have the bottom heat.

MB   *Market gardening's loss was the Irish theatre's gain, and thank goodness you came back because I think after that period* The Gigli Concert *was the next major play that you wrote, is that true?*

TM   No, I wrote *The Blue Macushla.*

MB   The Blue Macushla *came next, but I was leading towards* The Gigli Concert *as the next play produced in the season. I remember vividly that original production on this stage in 1983 and it was an extraordinary event. It's extraordinary because of the image and the ideas: the image of an Irish millionaire going through a breakdown visiting this dynamatologist. It is very difficult to ask writers about starting points, but can you now recall what was the momentum for this play? Where did this play spring from in your imagination?*

TM   It is. It's always very difficult to pinpoint anything like that. I've given this answer before when asked where an idea comes from: it comes from somewhere between heaven and Woolworths. I remember ten years or more before the actual writing of *The Gigli Concert* I became very friendly with the

great Colin Blakely, a wonderful actor, alas no longer with us.
Colin was doing a play of mine *The Morning After Optimism*
here, and we drank a fair amount together. I'm not jealous of
any other writers, but then, in those days, I had an unbearable
envy of singers. I thought it was the only possible thing to do
in life; it was the only possible way to express oneself –
singing rather than being a musician. If you're a fiddler you
still have some sort of instrument in your hand, but the idea
of song emerging from people … My envy of singers was so
great that, prior to striking up this new friendship with Colin,
I couldn't bear to listen to them because the envy was very
strong. But Colin at the time was taking singing lessons from
one of our great singing teachers here, Veronica Dunne, and
he had these records of Caruso and Gigli, and we used to
listen to those. And I met Colin one day and he had – you
remember Colin's long face? – well it was much longer this
day because Ronnie Dunne had demoted him from tenor to
baritone and he fancied himself as the tenor. And from that I
began to listen to the great singers again, and I had this idea of
somebody who wanted to sing like a great tenor, and ten years
later when I began to think about it I said: so what, everybody
wants to sing. And then this character JPW an English man
happened. I think at the time I was quite sick to death of Irish
men, Irish characters in plays, being the poetic ones. When
JPW came along I deliberately made him more poetic. I'm
sure the English race will be eternally grateful to me for that.

I don't set out with any great plan to write a play: it's quite
an assault on the page, the blank page, to discover the play in
the process of doing it. But then as I progressed, I came to

wonder why this crazy outrageous notion of wanting to sing? And then there was the evolution from that to the idea that somebody has sold out spiritually. This would be again where I would have absorbed some of the politics of this country. This was the era of the developers, the terrible things that were done to buildings in Dublin, and those people came from small villages and towns and cities around the country. It was from this background that there emerged someone who, having sold his soul, now wants his soul back. That was something like the way the play evolved.

MB   *You said you discovered the play in the process of writing it. So a play for you is never a thesis or an argument to be developed; it doesn't start from a concept, it starts from a character or a mood?*

TM   Character or mood, yes.

MB   *And then it becomes an exploration of that character or mood, which seems to me the most common way of writing plays. Do you recognize there are other possible ways?*

TM   In the very first play that I was involved in, myself and my old friend Noel O'Donoghue wrote a one act play, and Noel's learning was devastating. We were 22 or 23 at the time, and he explained to me what a scenario was: it was a plan of a play in terms of scenes, you called scene one Scene One, you said who was in it and what they were going to talk about, and if someone else came in or if one of them left, you were in to scene two. And we worked out 32 or 33 scenes and stayed rigidly to that plan and it worked extremely well. This was a first for both of us, and usually with a first play the beginner goes down every hill and has to climb the next one, or goes up a cul-de-sac and finds he/she has to come back, but this kept us on the straight and narrow. For myself, though, I'm a short distance thinker; I can't plan that far ahead. I have to discover it and it becomes an adventure for me, an adventure made up greatly of nightmare because one gets oneself into terrible trouble.

MB   *So the play is an adventure, an exploration. But at the same time as a professional practising dramatist you presumably have your built-in sense of structure to keep you going. But that's on the subconscious level, is it?*

TM   Well obviously there is a lot on the subconscious level. I know that I call myself a playwright; I know that I am writing lines that are going to be spoken by actors; I know that for myself, the actors and everybody involved we are dependent on audiences who will listen or not listen or watch these things. That kind of thing is inbuilt. But I find that it is nothing to me to do thirty drafts of a play – I mean from first word to last word. And the structure emerges, maybe it starts to emerge when I've got most of my material. The structuring happens much later, and I'm happy with that because if I start with the structure then I have to fit character and thought and excitement to that structure. I don't want to straightjacket it, but I've still got fifteen drafts to go to get the final structure of the thing.

MB   *You talked a moment ago about envy of singers which leads us on to music which is an integral part of all your work. I was noticing it yesterday when watching your production of* Bailegangaire, *how important music is in the subtext of that play, with the radio on almost throughout. Could you talk about the function of music in that play? Is the music there to heighten mood, or is it there also to provide a background of normalcy?*

TM   Normalcy, yes. It's a Sunday evening. I find when I go to plays sometimes they're staged in such a fashion that they're happening in a complete vacuum, and that certain plays require external noises like cars passing. There is another world happening out there. These three women in *Bailegangaire* are like forgotten people: it's 1984 – no Big Brother is watching these three people. The radio in that case is not there to heighten the drama; maybe at the end, I wanted to achieve an effect when Schubert's *Notturno* is fed in on practically the last words of the piece. But again maybe it is envy of the composer. Words, literature, writing drama is such a linear thing, whereas when I listen to music, I hear emotion, I hear mood; when I listen to the sound that people are making, I hear emotion and character. 'All art aspires to the condition of music'. The aspiration is to get a simultaneity of things happening, not to confuse the situation or make it over complex, but to get the richness of music that it is not just a linear point going from A to D or A to Z. In music you can be elated, deflated, happy, sad in a phrase of music. I try to write in a certain way, combining words in a certain way, varying rhythms, or seeking to continue a certain rhythm or repeat a certain rhythm, as a composer would a phrase of music to get what I think is a better form of drama.

MB   *What is instantly striking about that play is the fact that it's three women. How difficult is it ever for any male dramatist to fully understand and comprehend female psychology? Is it a different task altogether writing a play like that?*

TM   It is. The line of least resistance for me is to write male characters. Somebody I think said that in the whole canon of drama in the world 7% of the roles are for women. I suppose this is because the playwrights have been male. I was conscious over my career as a playwright of this: I'm fascinated by the idea of writing for women. One reason is that if I write for a woman I can more easily conceal personal emotions and feelings: that is a credit side. But this thing of writing for women started for me on my first first night ever when a woman came up to me and said, "Well done but if you don't mind my saying so you know nothing about women". So that has stuck in my mind, and in *Famine* I think I wrote a creditable mother character and perhaps Rosie in *The Morning After Optimism*. But when I came to do *Bailegangaire*, until the second or third last draft there was a male character in it, a very good character. Still, I thought it would be better if I could achieve the thing with just the three women. I was also conscious that I have generally observed the Aristotelian unities of time, action, place, and I thought I would introduce a fourth, gender.

MB   *But writing about women – obviously it comes from observation and understanding – does it also come from tapping into a different side of your own nature, the female side of you?*

TM   Possibly, I can't be sure. I don't keep a notebook, I absorb, but I know when the characters start to work for me I can create their distinctive and individual patterns of speech.

And similarly I think to achieve a degree of relaxation in the business of writing I need to start thinking women. One example: you can leave something on that table which will be the equivalent of a gauntlet, and if a male antagonist comes in he will go for the gauntlet or pick up the gauntlet straight away. If a woman comes in she will say, 'In my own time will I look at that' and move about it until it suits her.

MB *We'll probably have to stop talking in a moment, but there are just two or three other topics I'd like to bring up. One thing strikes me very much about your career – I know you've written fiction and I know you have written for television – but your career has been very much a career in the theatre: you are a writer of the theatre and for the theatre and your realm is the theatre. That is unusual in this day and age, when writers more and more seem to be gadding from medium to medium and fitting in a play when they're not writing a film script and so on. You seem to have a consistent love for and need for the theatre. Could you explain why? You talked about emotions – do you have great faith in the theatre as a medium for making emotional contact with a group of strangers, with an audience?*

TM I think that my instinct is predominantly for theatre. I've mentioned that I like to write the aria which isn't an aria that stops the action of a play. But I love dialogue and I love working with actors and for actors. I think it is the medium that suits me best. I think that were I a novelist I couldn't be repeating certain pursuits that I've repeated in plays like the flight from home in search of another home. It's very interesting to me to create different characters with different backgrounds, different nationalities, who are adrift in the world, who are abject, who are broken for whatever reason, and who are going into the abyss. The nature of theatre suits me for that. I find that in this search for home it's maybe as ordinary as in the animal kingdom where you have flight or fight: my characters seem to fly but then come back to fight. The other thing the animal does is play dead, and that is something I haven't done, or I don't want to do, because I suppose if one followed that pattern of playing dead one might arrive at a safe play or a dead play.

MB *Which your plays certainly are not. But to round off the discussion, are you conscious of the figure in the carpet, as it were? When you look at the huge and substantial body of your work and look at the retrospective season in this theatre, are you conscious of these recurring patterns, these recurring things? You've mentioned themes like the key one, flight from and search for home: is that the very essence to you of the work?*

TM It really isn't for me to say ... consciously, yes. I feel that reality, as it is, is unbearable because it's inadequate to deal with whatever the spirit of man is looking for. I feel that religion has not at all fulfilled a need that is within us all. I've said on occasion that I cannot face reality – that isn't quite true. I think that what I'm trying to do is look for a better reality which caters for this lostness, this longing that is within us all.

MB *It's a very pregnant statement, reality is unbearable. Is there any solution to this? You talked about socialism, didn't you, and you said socialism is an ideal way to organize society; you imply religion hasn't found the way. Is there any solution in the world to make our individual lives better?*

TM   Well one way I think is accepting that it is a valley of tears, and as is said in *Bailegangaire*, 'And sure a tear isn't such a bad thing?' I don't want to be offensive to American people, but there is an attitude in America, the denial of anything that is sad. And I think that as there is day, there is night and as there is depression there is elation. I don't have any political resolution or anything like that: maybe I found my way of passing the time by writing these plays.

BM   *That's a very Beckettian statement, I must say, to introduce a name we haven't mentioned once in the conversation ... I would like to say my personal thank you to Tom Murphy for being such a gracious and articulate and amusing and informative guest; thank you, Tom, very much indeed, not only for the plays but also for the conversation.*

TM   In my turn, I'd like to thank Michael Billington for being so gracious and for being such a painless interviewer. Thank you.

Contributors

Michael Billington is the Theatre Critic of *The Guardian* who has published many books on contemporary British theatre including *Alan Ayckbourn* (1983), *Stoppard: the Playwright* (1987), *Peggy Ashcroft* (1988) and *The Life and Work of Harold Pinter* (1996).

Nicholas Grene is Professor of English Literature at Trinity College, Dublin. His special interests are in Shakespeare and in modern Irish drama; his recent books include *The Politics of Irish Drama* (1999), *Interpreting Synge: Essays from the Synge Summer School* (2000), and *Shakespeare's Serial History Plays* (2002).

Declan Kiberd is Professor of Anglo-Irish Literature and Drama at University College Dublin. An international authority in his field, he has lectured in more than 20 countries; his books include *Synge and the Irish Language* (1979), *Men and Feminism in Modern Lierature* (1985) and the award-winning *Inventing Ireland* (1995) and *Irish Classics* (2000).

Chris Morash is Senior Lecturer in English at NUI Maynooth. He is the author of *A History of Irish Theatre: 1601-2000* (Cambridge, 2002) and *Writing the Irish Famine* (Oxford, 1995), the editor of several other books and numerous articles on Irish culture. He is also Consultant Editor on Theatre for the forthcoming *Encyclopaedia of Ireland*.

Tom Murphy has long been recognized as one of Ireland's outstanding playwrights from the success of his first full-length play *A Whistle in the Dark* (Theatre Royal, Stratford East, 1961) to his most recent *The House* (Abbey Theatre, 2000). Six of his plays were produced by the Abbey in a special season of his work in October 2001. He has served on the Board of the Abbey Theatre, is a member of Aosdána and of the Irish Academy of Letters; he has been awarded honorary degrees by both Trinity College, Dublin and the National University of Ireland.

Fintan O'Toole is one of Ireland's leading political and cultural commentators. Born in Dublin in 1958, he has been drama critic of *In Dublin* magazine, *The Sunday Tribune*, the New York *Daily News*, and *The Irish Times* and Literary Adviser to the Abbey Theatre. He edited *Magill* magazine and since 1988 has been a columnist with *The Irish Times*. Books include *The Irish Times Book of the Century* (1999); *A Traitor's Kiss: The Life of Richard Brinsley Sheridan* (1997); *The Lie of the Land: Selected Essays* (1997); *The Ex-Isle of Erin* (1996); *Black Hole, Green Card* (1994); *Meanwhile Back at the Ranch* (1995); *A Mass for Jesse James* (1990) and *The Politics of Magic: The Work and Times of Tom Murphy* (1987).

Lionel Pilkington is a lecturer in English at NUI, Galway. He is a co-editor of *Gender and Colonialism* (Galway: Galway University Press, 1995) and author of *Theatre and the State in 20th Century Ireland: Cultivating the People* (London and New York: Routledge, 2001) as well as various articles on Ireland's theatre and cultural history.

Alexandra Poulain is a senior lecturer at the University of Paris-IV-Sorbonne where she teaches English and Irish Literature. She has translated plays by Tom Murphy, Tom Kilroy, Frank McGuinness and Colin Teevan and is currently working on a book on Tom Murphy's plays.

Shaun Richards is Professor of Irish Studies at Staffordshire University. He has published widely on Irish drama and cultural politics and is co-author of *Writing Ireland: Colonialism Nationalism and Culture* and the editor of the *Cambridge Companion to Modern Irish Drama*.

Publications by Carysfort Press

Theatre Talk

Voices of Irish Theatre Practitioners
edited by Lilian Chambers, Ger FitzGibbon and
Eamonn Jordan

A series of interviews/evaluations of the most
prominent playwrights, directors, designers,
actors and administrators in Irish Theatre.

ISBN 0-9534-2576-2   €20/$19 *

Seen and Heard

Six New Plays by Irish Women
edited with an introduction by Cathy Leeney

A rich and funny, moving and theatrically
exciting collection of plays by Mary Elizabeth
Burke-Kennedy, Síofra Campbell, Emma
Donoghue, Anne Le Marquand Hartigan,
Michelle Read and Dolores Walshe.

ISBN 0-9534-2573-8   €19/$18 *

Theatre of Sound

Radio and the Dramatic Imagination
by Dermot Rattigan

An innovative study of the challenges that radio
drama poses to the creative imagination of the
writer, the production team, and the listener..

ISBN 0-9534-2575-4   €20/$19 *

The Starving and October Song

Two Contemporary Irish Plays
by Andrew Hinds

The Starving, set during and after the siege of
Derry in 1689, is a moving and engrossing drama
of the emotional journey of two men.

October Song, a superbly written family drama
set in real time in pre-ceasefire Derry.

ISBN 0-9534-2574-6   €10.15/$9.50*

Theatre Stuff

Critical Essays on Contemporary Irish Theatre
edited by Eamonn Jordan

Best selling essays on the successes and debates
of contemporary Irish theatre at home and
abroad.

Contributors include: Thomas Kilroy, Declan
Hughes, Anna McMullan, Declan Kiberd, Deirdre
Mulrooney, Fintan O'Toole, Christopher Murray,
Caoimhe McAvinchey and Terry Eagleton.

ISBN 0-9534-2571-1   €19/$18 *

Publications by Carysfort Press

Urfaust

A new version of Goethe's early "Faust"
in Brechtian mode, by Dan Farrelly

This version is based on Brecht's irreverent and
daring re-interpretation of the German classic.

ISBN 0-9534257-0-3   €7.60/$7*

Under the Curse

Goethe's "Iphigenie auf Tauris",
in a new version by Dan Farrelly

The Greek myth of Iphigenie grappling with the
curse on the house of Atreus is brought vividly to
life. This version is currently being used in
Johannesburg to explore problems of ancestry,
religion, and Black African women's spirituality.

ISBN 0-9534-2572-X   €8.15/$7.50*

In Search of the South African Iphigenie

by Erika von Wietersheim & Dan Farrelly

Discussions of Goethe's "Iphigenie auf Tauris"
(Under the Curse) as relevant to women's issues
in modern South Africa: women in family and
public life; the force of women's spirituality;
experience of personal relationships; attitudes to
parents and ancestors; involvement with religion.

ISBN 0-9534-2578-9   €10.15/$9.50*

The Theatre of Marina Carr

"before rules was made",
edited by Anna McMullan and Cathy Leeney

Essays by leading commentators and
practitioners in theatre, placing Marina Carr's
work in the context of the current Irish and
international theatre scene. This book will
examine the creative dialogue between theatre
professionals, Carr's powerful plays, and their
audiences.

ISBN 0-9534-2577-0   2002

---

* Plus post and packing

General Editor: Dan Farrelly

Carysfort Press, 58 Woodfield, Scholarstown Road, Rathfarnham, Dublin 16, Republic of Ireland.
t: (353 1) 4937383 f: (353 1) 4069815 e: info@carysfortpress.com **www.carysfortpress.com**